ALL MY SONS

All My Sons was Arthur Miller's first successful play, preceding such well-known works as *Death of a Salesman* and *The Crucible*. It is a play about responsibility and the consequences of action. Joe Keller only learns how inter-related people and events are when he discovers that his own son was one of the victims of his dubious action in selling cracked cylinder heads for Air Force planes that subsequently crashed.

THE HEREFORD PLAYS
General Editor E. R. Wood

Arthur Miller

All My Sons

with an Introduction by
E. R. WOOD

Heinemann Educational Publishers
Halley Court, Jordan Hill, Oxford OX2 8EJ
Part of Harcourt Education

Heinemann is the registered trademark of Harcourt Educational Limited

ISBN: 978 0 435225 78 0

Printed in China by CTPS

Contents

INTRODUCTION

ARTHUR MILLER was born in New York in 1915. His family were of Austrian Jewish origin, but the Jewish element does not appear to have been important in his upbringing or environment. The Millers were prosperous manufacturers until they were ruined by the economic crisis which hit America in 1931. Thereafter, Arthur Miller grew up in poverty; he worked as an errand-boy in early mornings before going to school, where he did not distinguish himself. (His teachers could not remember him later.) After working for two years in an automobile parts warehouse, he had earned enough to be able to enter the University of Michigan, where he helped to maintain himself by various jobs. Working at different times as a waiter, a factory hand and a lorry driver has given him plenty of experience of hardship and adversity.

He entered the University to study economics and history, but he also took a course in playwriting, and within a short time had won three important prizes. After graduating in 1938 he made a living by writing radio scripts, and he completed a number of 'desk drawer plays'. His first Broadway play, *The Man Who Had All the Luck* (1944), ran for only one week; but his next, *All My Sons* (1947), was very successful, winning the New York Critics' Circle Award. *Death of a Salesman* (1949) established him as a major dramatist, and this and *The Crucible* (1953) are now acknowledged classics of the modern theatre.

Arthur Miller has not been a prolific playwright; his only other plays are an adaptation of Ibsen's *An Enemy of the People*, staged in 1950, *A Memory of Two Mondays* and *A View from the Bridge* (1955), *Incident at Vichy* and *After the Fall* (1965), and *The Price* (1968).

He has also written a novel, *Focus* (1945) and some short stories, a selection of which are included in *I Don't Need You Any More* (1967). Arthur Miller died in 2005.

Themes

In the Introduction to his *Collected Plays*, Arthur Miller describes the seed from which the play *All My Sons* grew:

> During an idle chat in my living-room, a pious lady from the Middle West told of a family in her neighbourhood which had been destroyed when the daughter turned the father in to the authorities on discovering that he had been selling defective machinery to the army. The war was then in full blast.

The playwright had only to change the daughter into a son, and he had the bare facts on which his imagination could work to create the situation and the plot. Arthur Miller has always been inspired by 'the wonder of how people got to be the way they are'. He had to imagine and understand the sort of man who could do such a thing and apparently escape for years from retribution or expiation; then he needed a family and neighbours. In a more superficial mind this could have remained a small town scandal with no wider significance; but Arthur Miller could not be interested in writing a mere crime play showing the stages by which the guilt of a wicked man was laid bare and finally punished; he sought an explanation of the man's conduct, and found it in the kind of society which throws up such men – a society which thrives when a war is in 'full blast', providing an urgent drive for industrial production at home, with consequent profits for those involved, at the same time as others are sacrificing their lives abroad in the common cause.

The pressures of production, stimulated by the desperate needs of a community at war, are not seen as a genuine excuse for Joe Keller's conduct, though they provide a climate in which he – and even some of his neighbours – could find it natural. Arthur Miller does not condone it: his interest is in how it could be reconciled with the nature of a decent man, a loving father and an amiable neighbour. The explanation lies in Miller's word 'unrelatedness'. Keller is unable to see his obligations and responsibilities, as an individual, to the community where he belongs. He could not *feel* the appalling human consequences of his actions until he knew that they included the death of his own son, Larry. By making excuses to himself, he could bear to think of twenty-one other pilots killed as a result of his supplying cracked cylinder heads for their planes: it is only at the end of the play that he is forced to realize that we all belong to one another, that the dead pilots were in a sense all his sons.

Related to this theme of the individual and the community are questions about crime and punishment which may provoke discussion; for no categorical answers are offered in the play. The crime of Joe Keller has been committed long before the play opens, and nothing can now be done to mitigate the damage which originally resulted. What, then, should happen to Keller? Is there any value in expiation? Would he 'redeem himself' by going to prison? Should he be forgiven? Miller's characters do not know; they keep asking each other what they should do. Is his crime less because he did it for his family? Did Ann and George do 'a terrible thing' when they cut off communication with their father because they believed him guilty? These questions cannot be usefully discussed as matters of abstract morality, apart from the people and circumstances of the play. Arthur Miller is always interested in ideas, but always as they arise from the problems of living human beings. He himself insists that the ideas in themselves are not the primary ingredient of a play. 'Idea is very important to me as a dramatist,' he has written, 'but I think it is time someone said that playwrights, including the greatest, have not been noted for the new ideas they have broached. . . . Surely there is no known philosophy which was first announced through a play, nor any ethical idea.' It is the characters who move us, and to Miller the play's idea, its essential meaning, is 'a unifying force empowering the artist to evoke a cogent emotional life on the stage'. It is this emotional life that matters, then. The truth or importance of the 'philosophy' is brought home to us through the reality of the characters, idea made flesh and blood.

Characters

Arthur Miller's interest in the 'wonder' of human beings is particularly stirred by emotions and tensions in family life, and especially in the relationship of father and sons. (Compare *Death of a Salesman*). Here and in general his attitude to his characters is coloured by his admiration for the rare person who does not walk away from problems, who can face them without compromising, without lying to himself, without being willing to 'settle for half'; though this does not wither up his compassion for the man who fails and knows his own inadequacy. Both these preoccupations are apparent in *All My Sons*.

In any play of importance we expect some development in the characters, either in the sense that we come to see more under the outer appearance or in the sense that they themselves change under the stress of events. In *All My Sons* the characters develop in both senses.

Joe Keller at first appears to be a wholly likeable man, self-made, practical, 'a man among men', an affectionate and reasonable father, a considerate husband. Where he is present, there is common sense and quite a bit of laughter. We come in time to see what lies beneath these first impressions, and Joe himself changes in that his eyes are opened to the world around him – indeed, the play cannot end until this happens.

Knowing him as we think we do at the beginning, we believe his version of what happened at his workshop, and we admire the frankness (for he says he has nothing to hide) with which he recalls the day when he came home from the penitentiary:

The story was, I pulled a fast one in getting myself exonerated. So I get out of my car, and walk down the street. But very slow. And with a smile. The beast! I was the beast, the guy who made twenty-one P-40s crash in Australia. Kid, walking down the street that day, I was as guilty as hell. Except I wasn't, and there was a court paper in my pocket to prove I wasn't, and I walked ... past ... the porches. Result? Fourteen months later I had one of the best shops in the state again, a respected man again, bigger than ever!

'Joe McGuts', as Chris comments with admiration!

Later we learn that the neighbours still think he pulled a fast one, but they enjoy his company and admire him for having been smart. He certainly is smart – at pulling wool over people's eyes, perhaps because he can pull it over his own. What a generous, sympathetic view he takes of the partner whom he has betrayed and left to take the punishment for them both!

> 'Just try to see it human, see it human,' he pleads with Ann. 'All of a sudden a batch comes out with a crack. That happens, that's the business. A fine, hairline crack. All right, so ... so he's a little man, your father, always scared of loud voices. What'll the Major say? Half a day's production shot ... What'll *I* say? You know what I mean. Human. So he takes out his tools and he ... covers over the cracks. All right ... that's bad, it's wrong, but that's what a little man does.'

Who would believe that the little man was only doing as he was told by the big man, who feigned sickness so that he could afterwards deny all responsibility?

Even George, who arrives like an avenging spirit fresh from hearing his father's version, meaning to reopen the whole case, falls under the old spell, finds he likes Joe (and Kate) still, and listens while Joe reminds him of other occasions in the past when his father did foolish things and then tried to blame somebody else. It all sounds plausible. (But how could Joe have the face to condemn Steve for the very fault he himself had committed – unless he is unconscious of it?) George would have been completely taken in by Joe's sympathy, if Kate had not blundered into mentioning a detail (Joe's immunity to illness) that contradicted the version of the past which he had been ready to believe.

As for Ann, she believes that Joe 'only wants everybody happy'. (She should try telling that to her father!)

'Joe Keller's trouble,' Arthur Miller has written,[*] 'is not that he cannot tell right from wrong, but that his cast of mind cannot admit that he, personally, has any viable connection with his world, his universe, or his society.' This may be all very well as an explanation of how he could give instructions for cracks in cylinder heads to be concealed, without considering how this private act could have tragic results in the world beyond his ken; it does not explain away the wrong he did to Steve; for surely he had 'a viable connection' with his own partner? His betrayal of his partner is a minor crime compared with the other in terms of its consequences, but in the sort of human terms which should be well within Joe's grasp it is unforgivable.

When he is forced to admit that he was responsible, he pleads that he did it for the family – and this is true. He was no capitalist war-profiteer seeking vast power or wealth, but a smallish business man afraid of ruin and looking forward to seeing his sons in the firm. He still does not *feel* guilty.

It is perhaps surprising that such a man can stir the compassion of the audience or reader, as he undoubtedly does at the end. Even when the truth is out, Joe does not understand the revulsion that his son suffers:

'You want me to go to gaol?' he demands of Chris. 'If you want me to go, say so. I'll tell you why you can't say it. Because you know I don't belong there.'

On the level of personal guilt, surely he belongs there instead of Steve? But he defends his role in the community, and argues that in war time everybody is working for profit, and so is entitled (he implies) to sell cracked cylinders if the alternative is cancelled contracts:

'Who worked for nothing in that war?. . . Did they ship a gun or a tank outa Detroit before they got their price? Is that clear? It's dollars and cents, nickels and dimes; war and peace, it's

* Introduction to *Collected Plays*.

nickels and dimes. Half the goddam country is gotta go if I go!'
He is bewildered that this sort of attack should be levelled at him:
'Then ... why am I bad?'

The terrible clash with Chris is not enough to awaken his
conscience to what he has done. He still evades responsibility,
taking refuge now in disparaging the unpractical idealism that he
sees in Chris, and clinging to his belief that Larry would have
backed him up. 'He understood the way the world is made....
This one, everything bothers him. You make a deal, overcharge
two cents, and his hair falls out. He don't understand money....
But Larry! That was a boy we lost.'

Since family has always been everything to him, he has always
had to insist – and feel sure – that he could not possibly have been
responsible for the death of his own son. When he is forced to
realize, from reading Larry's last letter, that he was, and when he
knows what Larry thought of him at the end, he dully gropes
towards understanding his own guilt. He admits that Larry was
right: 'I think to him they were all my sons. And I guess they were,
I guess they were.'

Ever since the truth began to come out, he has been at a loss,
asking stumbling questions: 'What do I do? Tell me, talk to
me, what do I do?' Now at last he knows what to do and he
does it.

Keller's wife is described by the author as 'a woman of uncontrolled inspirations and an overwhelming capacity for love'.
As Keller's guilt is progressively revealed to us in the play, a
question of great interest is how much his wife knew of it.
Ultimately it becomes clear that she has known all about it. She
has probably suffered much more than he has. Early in the play
she gives us a glimpse of sensitive scars when she turns angrily on
him for playing police games with little Bert: 'I want you to stop
that, Joe. That whole gaol business!' Joe is astonished at her outburst, and quite uncomprehending. 'What have I got to hide?'
he asks, unaware. 'What the hell is the matter with you, Kate?'
He is concerned about her, for she is shaking, unable to control

herself. At other times, too, he is anxious for her, because what has happened has upset her so much more than him.

She has accepted his crime, but we do not know how she took it at the time. It is possible that her repeated warnings now that he will have to be smart (for instance when George is on his way to see them, certainly not with a blessing from his father), are echoes of past occasions when her misgivings were confidently brushed aside by Joe.

The one thing she could not face was Larry's death. She does not reason, as Keller did, about whether Larry ever flew the type of plane involved in the swindle: intuition tells her that if Larry is dead his father killed him. Therefore she will not accept that Larry is dead. 'As long as you live,' she tells Chris, 'that boy is alive. God does not let a son be killed by his father.' From this insistence, essential as it is to the fabric of her life and her universe, comes her obstinate opposition to Ann as a possible wife for Chris. She is fond of Ann, but suspicious; in resisting the marriage she is ruthless. Her intuition is probably right, anyhow, in prompting her forecast that a sense of guilt would cast a shadow over their happiness, for Chris is afflicted by a sense of guilt for having survived the war when others were killed, and for having returned to the rat-race where nobody has changed; and they both will think of Larry.

The non-rational mental processes by which she rejects Larry's death are common in her make-up: she has a dream about Larry which coincides with the destruction of Larry's tree, and she sees significance in the arrival of Larry's girl on the same night. She recalls that she had some kind of telepathic awareness of danger to Chris – and she was right – once during the war. This is of a piece with her encouragement of Frank's dabblings in astrology, which confirm her logic of evasion: if the date of Larry's death was a fortunate day astrologically for him, then he cannot have been killed.

But, although she says she is stupid, she is not. Her 'uncontrolled inspirations' and 'overwhelming capacity for love' combine to make her the warmest and in some ways the wisest person in the play. The way she talks to George, Chris, and even Ann, is prompted not so much by reason as by human feeling. Above all, her behaviour to Joe, varying from fractious rebukes to deep anxiety for him, comes from her love. She has an intuitive understanding of what is wrong in his life, and finally of what must be done. 'You ought to make it clear to him (Chris) that you know you did a terrible thing. . . . I mean, if he saw you realize what you did. . . . You see?' She is absolutely right. Beyond this, she feels that when Joe has killed himself, the burden is lifted; Chris must not take it on himself. 'Forget now,' she urges him. 'Live.' She is surely right again.

She has not had a comfortable life with Joe. Whenever there was trouble he yelled at her, she says, and thought that settled it. But she understood him, stood by him and protected him. His life has been hers. Those who were against him were against her. She has accepted the whole of him, not merely the good parts. That is what love means.

If it was right that Kate should stand by Joe Keller for better or worse, how are we to regard the bitter rejection of father by son? It happens twice to Keller, once by Larry and again by Chris. Chris is a man 'capable of immense affection and loyalty', the author says, and the father-son relationship offers scope for both. 'There's nothing I wouldn't forgive him,' says Keller about Chris, 'because he's my son.' But in the case of Chris the relationship works the other way; it is just because Keller is his father that Chris is so brutally shocked by the truth about him. 'I know you're no worse than other men,' he says, 'but I thought you were better. I never saw you as a man. I saw you as my father.' The bitterness of his disillusionment is reinforced by self-contempt, not for having been deceived, but for having half-suspected and done nothing about it.

Another reason why he reacts so angrily, and so differently from his mother, lies in his experience of the war. He had seen so much self-sacrifice among his soldiers that he was filled with a special loathing of the money-grubbers at home. While Keller was worrying about the danger of being pushed out of business, Chris was commanding a company of men who were giving their lives for the common good. 'And I got an idea, watching them go down. Everything was being destroyed, see, but it seemed to me that one new thing was being made. A kind of responsibility. Man for man.' When he came back from the war he found that nobody at home was changed at all; the war had meant no more to them than a kind of bus accident. 'It seemed to make suckers out of a lot of guys.'

Chris had settled uneasily into his father's business, unwilling to commit himself fully by having his name added to the firm, still not understanding, according to his father, 'how a buck is made', but fond and proud of his father. When his mother lets out how far his father could descend in the interests of business, Chris has to face it. Under fierce cross-examination, Keller pleads that he did it all for him. Then the outraged idealist turns on the old swindler: 'Is that as far as your mind can see, the business? What the hell do you mean, you did it for me? Don't you have a country? Don't you live in the world? What the hell are you? You're not even an animal; no animal kills his own. What are you? What must I do to you?' His revulsion from his father is as brutal as Larry's.

Chris has hitherto half-evaded the truth that was half-formed in his mind; he has compromised more than he has admitted to himself. Now he cannot walk away from the problem. But he does not know what to do. He says that he is yellow, that he ought to send his father to gaol, but they have made him 'practical'. He knows, though, that going to gaol will solve nothing. Keller has to change in himself. 'You can be better,' he tells his mother. 'Once and for all you can know there's a universe of people outside, and you're responsible to it.'

The actor playing Chris needs to watch the danger of making him sound self-righteous. Ann says of him: 'Whenever I need somebody to tell me the truth, I've always thought of Chris.

When he tells you something you know it's so.' But Sue (who says she resents living next door to the Holy Family) complains: 'Chris makes people want to be better than it's possible to be.' She is cynical about Keller's exoneration and about Chris's high moral principles: 'Chris is working with his father, isn't he? He's taking money out of the business every week in the year.' Keller also protests against his son's exacting standards: 'Chris, a man can't be Jesus in this world!' (The name Christopher means 'Christ-bearer', but his parents may not have thought of its meaning when they gave him that name.) One recoils a little from the sentimentality of his picture of army life in his company, of how one youngster gave him his only pair of dry socks. . . . 'That's only a little thing but . . . that's the kind of guys I had. They didn't die: they killed themselves for each other.' The part needs to be played so that we don't approve when Sue says, 'If Chris wants people to put on the hair shirt let him take off his broadcloth. He's driving my husband crazy with that phony idealism of his.' His idealism is not phoney: it is frustrated, questing, struggling for survival in an alien world. A suspicion of priggishness may threaten people who try to uphold morality in a world of com-promisers if they are too sure they are right: Chris is saved from this by uncertainty, self-doubt, humility.

The family situation of Ann and George is parallel to that of Chris and Larry, though their father was evidently a lesser man than Keller. Ann has not always been so cold towards her father: when she knew that he had been found guilty of an act that caused the deaths of twenty-one pilots, she went to see him in prison on every visiting day: she turned her back on him forever only when the news came about Larry. This suggests that her imagina-tion remained inert while the victims were merely unknown pilots, but brought the crime home to her as soon as it involved somebody who mattered to her. It is a more extreme case of what happened to Kate. She is more implacable than her brother. George did at least go to see his father to tell him that Ann was thinking of getting married (though the news was surely premature?); once he saw him he pitied him and believed him. Ann is not moved to change her attitude; anyhow, her mind is on marrying into the family whose guts her father understandably hates. Moreover, George also has second thoughts in the friendly atmosphere created by Joe and Kate, whom he always liked. We, who know that Steve was not the bearer of prime responsibility for the crime, are inclined to agree with George that he and Ann did a terrible thing to their father. Even if he was wholly guilty, they should have treated him as a human being. But the young tend to be rigid in such things. Ann develops more understanding as the play proceeds, showing some forbearance towards Joe, though she is torn different ways and carries all the time the letter from Larry that clinches the whole extent of guilt. At least she is willing to build bridges in the Keller territory, and that is not easy to do with Kate.

An interesting and sympathetic character is Dr Jim Bayliss, who understands from his own experience how Chris suffers, and who knows about Joe, but accepts him, not out of cynical indifference to wrong, as his wife Sue does, but out of humanity. He has had ideals once about what he ought to do with his life, but he has had to settle for half. 'It's even hard sometimes to remember the kind of man I used to be.' He is afraid that Chris may be watching his star – the star of honesty – go out; for he knows that most of us compromise in the end. He may be too pessimistic about Chris, but he knows his own weakness.

Dramatic Qualities

All My Sons has some of the old-fashioned virtues that are conspicuous in the work of Ibsen, whose influence Arthur Miller readily acknowledges, though with some qualification. One common feature is the method of telling the story: Ibsen likes to begin his play at a point near the end of a chain of events, and he shows great skill in bringing the past back to life so that it explains and dominates the present. Miller follows the same pattern, though he recognizes that in the modern theatre it is no longer in favour. 'Anyone making a study of some highly creditable plays of the moment.' he writes,* 'would be hard put to imagine what their characters were like a month before their actions and stories begin. *All My Sons* takes its time with the past, not in deference to Ibsen's method as I saw it then, but because its theme is the question of actions and consequences, and a way had to be found to throw a long line into the past in order to make that connection viable.' So in *All My Sons* we begin with an apparently calm surface, which is gradually shown to conceal disturbing tensions, until the ugly truth about what happened years ago is laid bare with tragic results. By the time we reach the end of the play it has become possible to re-construct the story of what Keller did, beginning with the arrival of the cracked cylinder heads in his workshop, and showing the chain of consequences, some unforeseen, some unacknowledged and some unknown to him until the end. Such a chronological account would be much less dramatic; for the Ibsenite method, whether the actual theme of a play is explicitly the same as Miller's or not, produces a special dramatic excitement.

Once you have learnt from a first hearing or reading of the play what happens on the stage and what has happened in the past to create this situation and these characters, you will be ready to appreciate the skill with which the past is probed, in conversation and behaviour that appears realistic. Notice, for example, how credibly the broken tree is used to initiate explorations of the past. Frank asks what has happened to it, wonders what Kate will say, associates it with Larry, who (it emerges) was reported missing in the war, but may possibly be still alive; Kate connects it with her nightmare of Larry's crash, and so it leads forward to Chris telling his mother she must accept the death of Larry, which is related to the coming clash over his marriage to Ann. Looking over the play we can see other details falling into place and serving a future purpose; for example, Keller's game with Bert first brings up mention of gaols and provokes a significant

* In the Introduction to *Collected Plays*.

outburst from Kate which we do not understand at the time. It makes us aware of tension beneath the surface, something that is exciting in the theatre, but also true of real life, which is dangerously haunted, both for peoples and for individuals, by events of long ago.*

Another virtue of the drama of Ibsen's age, less conspicuous and less admired in the theatre of today, is the shaping of the tensions and outright clashes, into climaxes of mounting intensity, designed so as to ensure that each act ends with an effective curtain. So too in *All My Sons* the quiet opening, with its deceptive atmosphere of geniality and even fun, develops with apparent progress through potential emotional minefields until an unexpected phone call from George promises an urgent and disturbing challenge. The second act builds up through more open conflicts to the crisis in which Chris, realizing the truth at last exclaims: 'Dad . . . Dad, you killed twenty-one men!' He has still to make his father admit the wrong he did, and the resulting exchanges are very reminiscent of those intensely dramatic occasions in courts of law when the accused, obstinately maintaining that he didn't know he was doing wrong, is broken down in crossexamination by an inexorable prosecuting counsel:

COUNSEL FOR THE PROSECUTION: You knew the planes would not hold up in the air.
ACCUSED: I didn't say that.
COUNSEL: But you were going to warn them, you said, not to use them?
ACCUSED: But that don't mean . . .
COUNSEL: It means you knew they'd crash.
ACCUSED: It don't mean that.
COUNSEL: Then you *thought* they'd crash?
ACCUSED: I was afraid maybe . . .

* Contrast this concealed technique with the crude contrivance by which Shakespeare in *The Tempest* makes Prospero relate to his daughter, at such length that she keeps falling asleep, the wrongs inflicted on him fourteen years before, which he is now in a position to put right.

COUNSEL: You were afraid maybe!

Chris is more emotional than counsel would be: 'God in Heaven!' he shouts, 'What kind of a man are you?' The confrontation leads on to the culminating denunciation, ending with Chris hammering at his father with his fist, then stumbling away weeping and asking, 'What must I do, Jesus God, what must I do?' while his father makes broken distress signals: 'Chris . . . my Chris!'

This is very powerful drama indeed, because the emotional conflict is genuine, very moving and important to all of us; but also because it is directed into a shape which concentrates the theatrical experience to make the fullest impact. There can be no doubt in the minds of an audience that this is the end of a movement, but an interval of silence would seem more appropriate here than an adjournment for coffee, or for laughter in the theatre bar.

The three acts of classical drama deal with Exposition, Conflict and Catastrophe; and *All My Sons* admirably exemplifies this structure. In the last act Keller still has to be convinced that he was responsible for the death of his own son, and the playwright holds back until the last minutes the evidence of Larry's last letter. Readers or theatregoers brought up on the blurred conflicts and muffled climaxes of recent plays, often left indeterminate and shapeless on the plea that real life is indeterminate and shapeless, may decry the conscious craftmanship of the 'well-made play', and may cite the delayed production of the letter as an example of a contrived and unconvincing expedient. Why has Ann kept quiet about the letter for so long – unless to provide the author with a timely *coup de theatre*? Similarly some theatre-goers may deride the shot heard off-stage at the end, considering that this device has been used so often as to have become a theatrical cliché. As to the letter, Ann does explain why she has kept it back. As to the shot, it is in character and entirely appropriate; Keller's suicide is inevitable for him, and there is no reason why it should now be muted. Real life may be less tidy than the drama, but it is not necessarily falsified in essentials by being fitted into what is practicable and effective in the theatre. *All My Sons* observes more than most modern plays the disciplines once thought valuable, if not essential, in writing for the theatre; it even conforms with the three unities of time, place and action. It does not thereby lose in truth.

For Further Study

Arthur Miller's *Collected Plays* (Cresset Press, 1958) contains all his published plays except the last (*The Price*) and a long introduction by the author to the five plays included.

Arthur Miller: The Burning Glass, by Sheila Huftel (W. H. Allen, 1965) contains an admirable chapter on *All My Sons*.

Arthur Miller, by Ronald Hayman (Heinemann, Contemporary Playwrights Series, 1970) analyses *All My Sons* in a useful running commentary.

Arthur Miller, by Dennis Welland (Oliver and Boyd, Writers and Critics Series, 1961) has much of value to say about *All My Sons*, which is summed up as 'a social drama, not as an attack on the capitalist business ethic, but as a study of the bewildered common man groping in a world where moral values have become a shifting quicksand, where you ask for guidance from others no surer than yourself, and where the simplest lesson – moral responsibility to others – is the hardest to learn'.

CAST OF FIRST LONDON PERFORMANCE

All My Sons received its first London performance at the Lyric, Hammersmith on 11 May 1948 and transferred to the Globe Theatre on 16 June 1948. The cast was as follows:

JOE KELLER	Joseph Calleia
DR JIM BAYLISS	Hugh Pryse
FRANK LUBEY	Peter Hutton
SUE BAYLISS	Louise Lister
LYDIA LUBEY	Barbara Todd
CHRIS KELLER	Richard Leech
BERT	Robin Netscher
KATE KELLER	Margalo Gillmere
ANN DEEVER	Harriette Johns
GEORGE DEEVER	John McLaren

The play was directed by Warren Jenkins.

CHARACTERS

JOE KELLER
KATE KELLER
CHRIS KELLER
ANN DEEVER
GEORGE DEEVER
DR JIM BAYLISS
SUE BAYLISS
FRANK LUBEY
LYDIA LUBEY
BERT

ALL MY SONS

ACT ONE

The back yard of the Keller home in the outskirts of an American town. August of our era.

The stage is hedged on right and left by tall, closely planted poplars which lend the yard a secluded atmosphere. Upstage is filled with the back of the house and its open, unroofed porch which extends into the yard some six feet. The house is two stories high and has seven rooms. It would have cost perhaps fifteen thousand in the early twenties when it was built. Now it is nicely painted, looks tight and comfortable, and the yard is green with sod, here and there plants whose season is gone. At the right, beside the house, the entrance of the driveway can be seen, but the poplars cut off view of its continuation downstage. In the left corner, downstage, stands the four-foot-high stump of a slender apple tree whose upper trunk and branches lie toppled beside it, fruit still clinging to its branches.

Downstage right is a small, trellised arbour, shaped like a sea shell, with a decorative bulb hanging from its forward-curving roof. Garden chairs and a table are scattered about. A garbage pail on the ground next to the porch steps, a wire leaf-burner near it.

On the rise: It is early Sunday morning. JOE KELLER *is sitting in the sun reading the want ads of the Sunday paper, the other sections of which lie neatly on the ground beside him. Behind his back, inside the arbour,* DOCTOR JIM BAYLISS *is reading part of the paper at the table.*

KELLER *is nearing sixty. A heavy man of stolid mind and build, a business man these many years, but with the imprint of the machine-shop worker and boss still upon him. When he reads, when he speaks, when he listens, it is with the terrible concentration of the uneducated man for whom there is still wonder in many commonly known things, a man whose judgements must be dredged out of experience and a peasant-like common sense. A man among men.*

DOCTOR BAYLISS *is nearly forty. A wry self-controlled man, an easy talker, but with a wisp of sadness that clings even to his self-effacing humour.*

At curtain, JIM *is standing at left, staring at the broken tree. He taps a pipe on it, blows through the pipe, feels in his pockets for tobacco, then speaks.*

JIM: Where's your tobacco?

KELLER: I think I left it on the table. (JIM *goes slowly to table on the arbour, finds a pouch, and sits there on the bench, filling his pipe.*) Gonna rain tonight.

JIM: Paper says so?

KELLER: Yeah, right here.

JIM: Then it can't rain.

    FRANK LUBEY *enters, through a small space between the poplars. Frank is thirty-two but balding. A pleasant opinionated man, uncertain of himself, with a tendency towards peevishness when crossed, but always wanting it pleasant and neighbourly. He rather saunters in, leisurely, nothing to do. He does not notice Jim in the arbour. On his greeting, Jim does not bother looking up.*

FRANK: Hya.

KELLER: Hello, Frank. What's doin'?

FRANK: Nothin'. Walking off my breakfast. (*Looks up at the sky.*) That beautiful? Not a cloud.

KELLER (*looking up*): Yeah, nice.

FRANK: Every Sunday ought to be like this.

KELLER (*indicating the sections beside him*): Want the paper?

FRANK: What's the difference, it's all bad news. What's today's calamity?

KELLER: I don't know. I don't read the news part any more. It's more interesting in the want ads.

FRANK: Why, you trying to buy something?

KELLER: No, I'm just interested. To see what people want,

y'know? For instance, here's a guy is lookin' for two Newfoundland dogs. Now what's he want with two Newfoundland
dogs?

FRANK: That is funny.

KELLER: Here's another one. Wanted – old dictionaries. High
prices paid. Now what's a man going to do with an old
dictionary?

FRANK: Why not? Probably a book collector.

KELLER: You mean he'll make a living out of that?

FRANK: Sure, there's a lot of them.

KELLER (*shaking his head*): All the kind of business goin' on. In my
day, either you were a lawyer, or a doctor, or you worked in a
shop. Now —

FRANK: Well, I was going to be a forester once.

KELLER: Well, that shows you; in my day, there was no such
thing. (*Scanning the page, sweeping it with his hand.*) You look at
a page like this you realize how ignorant you are. (*Softly, with
wonder, as he scans page.*) Psss!

FRANK (*noticing tree*): Hey, what happened to your tree?

KELLER: Ain't that awful? The wind must've got it last night.
You heard the wind, didn't you?

FRANK: Yeah, I got a mess in my yard, too. (*Goes to tree.*) What a
pity. (*Turning to Keller.*) What'd Kate say?

KELLER: They're all asleep yet. I'm just waiting for her to see it.

FRANK (*struck*): You know? – it's funny.

KELLER: What?

FRANK: Larry was born in August. He'd been twenty-seven this
month. And his tree blows down.

KELLER (*touched*): I'm surprised you remember his birthday,
Frank. That's nice.

FRANK: Well, I'm working on his horoscope.

KELLER: How can you make him a horoscope? That's for the
future, ain't it?

FRANK: Well, what I'm doing is this, see. Larry was reported
missing on November twenty-fifth, right?

KELLER: Yeah?

FRANK: Well, then, we assume that if he was killed it was on November twenty-fifth. Now, what Kate wants —

KELLER: Oh, Kate asked you to make a horoscope?

FRANK: Yeah, what she wants to find out is whether November twenty-fifth was a favourable day for Larry.

KELLER: What is that, favourable day?

FRANK: Well, a favourable day for a person is a fortunate day, according to his stars. In other words it would be practically impossible for him to have died on his favourable day.

KELLER: Well, was that his favourable day? – November twenty-fifth?

FRANK: That's what I'm working on to find out. It takes time! See, the point is, if November twenty-fifth was his favourable day, then it's completely possible he's alive somewhere, because – I mean it's possible. (*He notices Jim now.* JIM *is looking at him as though at an idiot. To Jim – with an uncertain laugh.*) I didn't even see you.

KELLER (*to Jim*): Is he talkin' sense?

JIM: Him? He's all right. He's just completely out of his mind, that's all.

FRANK (*peeved*): The trouble with you is, you don't *believe* in anything.

JIM: And your trouble is that you believe in *anything*. *You* didn't see my kid this morning, did you?

FRANK: No.

KELLER: Imagine! He walked off with his thermometer. Right out of his bag.

JIM (*getting up*): What a problem. One look at a girl and he takes her temperature. (*Goes to driveway, looks upstage towards street.*)

FRANK: That boy's going to be a real doctor; he's smart.

JIM: Over my dead body he'll be a doctor. A good beginning, too.

FRANK: Why? It's an honourable profession.

JIM (*looking at him tiredly*): Frank, will you stop talking like a civics book? (*Keller laughs.*)

FRANK: Why, I saw a movie a couple of weeks ago, reminded me of you. There was a doctor in that picture —

KELLER: Don Ameche!

FRANK: I think it was, yeah. And he worked in his basement discovering things. That's what you ought to do; you could help humanity, instead of —

JIM: I would love to help humanity on a Warner Brothers salary.

KELLER (*pointing at him, laughing*): That's very good, Jim.

JIM (*looking towards house*): Well, where's the beautiful girl was supposed to be here?

FRANK (*excited*): Annie came?

KELLER: Sure, sleepin' upstairs. We picked her up on the one o'clock train last night. Wonderful thing. Girl leaves here, a scrawny kid. Couple of years go by, she's a regular woman. Hardly recognized her, and she was running in and out of this yard all her life. That was a very happy family used to live in your house, Jim.

JIM: Like to meet her. The block can use a pretty girl. In the whole neighbourhood there's not a damned thing to look at. (SUE, *Jim's wife, enters. She is rounding forty, an overweight woman who fears it. On seeing her* JIM *wryly adds.*) Except my wife, of course.

SUE (*in same spirit*): Mrs Adams is on the phone, you dog.

JIM (*to Keller*): Such is the condition which prevails —(*going to his wife*) my love, my light.

SUE: Don't sniff around me. (*Pointing to their house.*) And give her a nasty answer. I can smell her perfume over the phone.

JIM: What's the matter with her now?

SUE: I don't know, dear. She sounds like she's in terrible pain – unless her mouth is full of candy.

JIM: Why don't you just tell her to lay down?

SUE: She enjoys it more when you tell her to lay down. And when are you going to see Mr Hubbard?

JIM: My dear, Mr Hubbard is not sick, and I have better things to do than to sit there and hold his hand.

SUE: It seems to me that for ten dollars you could hold his hand.

JIM (*to Keller*): If your son wants to play golf tell him I'm ready. Or if he'd like to take a trip around the world for about thirty years. (*He exits.*)

KELLER: Why do you needle him? He's a doctor, women are supposed to call him up.

SUE: All I said was Mrs Adams is on the phone. Can I have some of your parsley?

KELLER: Yeah, sure. (*She goes to parsley box and pulls some parsley.*) You were a nurse too long, Susie. You're too ... too ... realistic.

SUE (*laughing, pointing at him*): Now you said it!

   LYDIA LUBEY *enters, She is a robust, laughing girl of twenty-seven.*

LYDIA: Frank, the toaster – (*Sees the others.*) Hya.

KELLER: Hello!

LYDIA (*to Frank*): The toaster is off again.

FRANK: Well, plug it in, I just fixed it.

LYDIA (*kindly, but insistently*): Please, dear, fix it back like it was before.

FRANK: I don't know why you can't learn to turn on a simple thing like a toaster! (*He exits.*)

SUE (*laughing*): Thomas Edison.

LYDIA (*apologetically*): He's really very handy. (*She sees broken tree.*) Oh, did the wind get your tree?

KELLER: Yeah, last night.

LYDIA: Oh, what a pity. Annie get in?

KELLER: She'll be down soon. Wait'll you meet her, Sue, she's a knockout.

SUE: I should've been a man. People are always introducing me to beautiful women. (*To Joe.*) Tell her to come over later: I imagine she'd like to see what we did with her house. And thanks. (*She exits.*)

LYDIA: Is she still unhappy, Joe?

KELLER: Annie? I don't suppose she goes around dancing on her toes, but she seems to be over it.

LYDIA: She going to get married? Is there anybody —?

KELLER: I suppose – say, it's a couple years already. She can't mourn a boy forever.

LYDIA: It's so strange – Annie's here and not even married. And I've got three babies. I always thought it'd be the other way around.

KELLER: Well, that's what a war does. I had two sons, now I got one. It changed all the tallies. In my day when you had sons it was an honour. Today a doctor could make a million dollars if he could figure out a way to bring a boy into the world without a trigger finger.

LYDIA: You know, I was just reading —

Enter CHRIS KELLER *from house, stands in doorway.*

LYDIA: Hya, Chris.

FRANK *shouts from offstage.*

FRANK: Lydia, come in here! If you want the toaster to work don't plug in the malted mixer.

LYDIA (*embarrassed, laughing*): Did I?

FRANK: And the next time I fix something don't tell me I'm crazy! Now come in here!

LYDIA (*to Keller*): I'll never hear the end of this one.

KELLER (*calling to Frank*): So what's the difference? Instead of toast have a malted!

LYDIA: Sh! sh! (*She exits, laughing.*)

CHRIS *watches her off. He is thirty-two; like his father, solidly built, a listener. A man capable of immense affection and loyalty. He has a cup of coffee in one hand, part of a doughnut in the other.*

KELLER: You want the paper?

CHRIS: That's all right, just the book section. (*He bends down and pulls out part of paper on porch floor.*)

KELLER: You're always reading the book section and you never buy a book.

CHRIS (*coming down to settee*): I like to keep abreast of my ignorance. (*He sits on settee.*)

KELLER: What is that, every week a new book comes out?

CHRIS: Lot of new books.

KELLER: All different.

CHRIS: All different.

   KELLER *shakes his head, puts knife down on bench, takes oilstone up to the cabinet.*

KELLER: Psss! Annie up yet?

CHRIS: Mother's giving her breakfast in the dining-room.

KELLER (*looking at broken tree*): See what happened to the tree?

CHRIS (*without looking up*): Yeah.

KELLER: What's Mother going to say?

   BERT *runs on from driveway. He is about eight. He jumps on stool, then on Keller's back.*

BERT: You're finally up.

KELLER (*swinging him around and putting him down*): Ha! Bert's here! Where's Tommy? He's got his father's thermometer again.

BERT: He's taking a reading.

CHRIS: What!

BERT: But it's only oral.

KELLER: Oh, well, there's no harm in oral. So what's new this morning, Bert?

BERT: Nothin'. (*He goes to broken tree, walks around it.*)

KELLER: Then you couldn't've made a complete inspection of the block. In the beginning, when I first made you a policeman you used to come in every morning with something new. Now, nothin's ever new.

BERT: Except some kids from Thirtieth Street. They started kicking a can down the block, and I made them go away because you were sleeping.

KELLER: Now you're talkin', Bert. Now you're on the ball. First thing you know I'm liable to make you a detective.

BERT (*pulling him down by the lapel and whispering in his ear*): Can I see the jail now?

KELLER: Seein' the jail ain't allowed, Bert. You know that.

BERT: Aw, I betcha there isn't even a jail. I don't see any bars on the cellar windows.

KELLER: Bert, on my word of honour there's a jail in the basement. I showed you my gun, didn't I?

BERT: But that's a hunting gun.

KELLER: That's an arresting gun!

BERT: Then why don't you ever arrest anybody? Tommy said another dirty word to Doris yesterday, and you didn't even demote him.

KELLER *chuckles and winks at Chris, who is enjoying all this.*

KELLER: Yeah, that's a dangerous character, that Tommy. (*Beckons him closer.*) What word does he say?

BERT (*backing away quickly in great embarrassment*): Oh, I can't say that.

KELLER (*grabbing him by the shirt and pulling him back*): Well, gimme an idea.

BERT: I can't. It's not a nice word.

KELLER: Just whisper it in my ear. I'll close my eyes. Maybe I won't even hear it.

BERT, *on tiptoe, puts his lips to Keller's ear, then in unbearable embarrassment steps back.*

BERT: I can't, Mr Keller.

CHRIS (*laughing*): Don't make him do that.

KELLER: Okay, Bert. I take your word. Now go out, and keep both eyes peeled.

BERT (*interested*): For what?

KELLER: For what! Bert, the whole neighbourhood is depending on you. A policeman don't ask questions. Now peel them eyes!

BERT (*mystified, but willing*): Okay. (*He runs off stage back of arbour.*)

KELLER (*calling after him*): And mum's the word, Bert.

BERT: About what?

KELLER: Just in general. Be v-e-r-y careful.

BERT (*nodding in bewilderment*): Okay. (*He exits.*)

KELLER (*laughing*): I got all the kids crazy!

CHRIS: One of these days, they'll all come in here and beat your brains out.

KELLER: What's she going to say? Maybe we ought to tell her before she sees it.

CHRIS: She saw it.

KELLER: How could she see it? I was the first one up. She was still in bed.

CHRIS: She was out here when it broke.

KELLER: When?

CHRIS: About four this morning. (*Indicating window above them.*) I heard it cracking and I woke up and looked out. She was standing right here when it cracked.

KELLER: What was she doing out here four in the morning?

CHRIS: I don't know. When it cracked she ran back into the house and cried in the kitchen.

KELLER: Did you talk to her?

CHRIS: No, I – I figured the best thing was to leave her alone. (*Pause.*)

KELLER (*deeply touched*): She cried hard?

CHRIS: I could hear her right through the floor of my room.

KELLER (*after slight pause*): What was she doing out here at that hour? (CHRIS *silent. With an undertone of anger showing.*) She's dreaming about him again. She's walking around at night.

CHRIS: I guess she is.

KELLER: She's getting just like after he died. (*Slight pause.*) What's the meaning of that?

CHRIS: I don't know the meaning of it. (*Slight pause.*) But I know one thing, Dad. We've made a terrible mistake with Mother.

KELLER: What?

CHRIS: Being dishonest with her. That kind of thing always pays off, and now it's paying off.

KELLER: What do you mean, dishonest?

CHRIS: You know Larry's not coming back and I know it. Why do we allow her to go on thinking that we believe with her?

KELLER: What do you want to do, argue with her?

CHRIS: I don't want to argue with her, but it's time she realized that nobody believes Larry is alive any more. (KELLER *simply moves away, thinking, looking at the ground.*) Why shouldn't she dream of him, walk the nights waiting for him? Do we contradict her? Do we say straight out that we have no hope any more? That we haven't had any hope for years now?

KELLER (*frightened at the thought*): You can't say that to her.

CHRIS: We've got to say it to her.

KELLER: How're you going to prove it? Can you prove it?

CHRIS: For God's sake, three years! Nobody comes back after three years. It's insane.

KELLER: To you it is, and to me. But not to her. You can talk yourself blue in the face, but there's no body and there's no grave, so where are you?

CHRIS: Sit down, Dad. I want to talk to you.

    KELLER *looks at him searchingly a moment.*

KELLER: The trouble is the Goddam newspapers. Every month some boy turns up from nowhere, so the next one is going to be Larry, so —

CHRIS: All right, all right, listen to me. (*Slight pause.* KELLER *sits on settee.*) You know why I asked Annie here, don't you?

KELLER (*he knows, but —*): Why?

CHRIS: You know.

KELLER: Well, I got an idea, but – What's the story?

CHRIS: I'm going to ask her to marry me. (*Slight pause.*)

    KELLER *nods.*

KELLER: Well, that's only your business, Chris.

CHRIS: You know it's not only my business.

KELLER: What do you want me to do? You're old enough to know your own mind.

CHRIS (*asking, annoyed*): Then it's all right, I'll go ahead with it?

KELLER: Well, you want to be sure Mother isn't going to —

CHRIS: Then it isn't just my business.

KELLER: I'm just sayin' —

CHRIS: Sometimes you infuriate me, you know that? Isn't it your business, too, if I tell this to Mother and she throws a fit about it? You have such a talent for ignoring things.

KELLER: I ignore what I gotta ignore. The girl is Larry's girl.

CHRIS: She's not Larry's girl.

KELLER: From Mother's point of view he is not dead and you have no right to take his girl. (*Slight pause.*) Now you can go on from there if you know where to go, but I'm tellin' you I don't know where to go. See? I don't know. Now what can I do for you?

CHRIS: I don't know why it is, but every time I reach out for something I want, I have to pull back because other people will suffer. My whole bloody life, time after time after time.

KELLER: You're a considerate fella, there's nothing wrong in that.

CHRIS: To hell with that.

KELLER: Did you ask Annie yet?

CHRIS: I wanted to get this settled first.

KELLER: How do you know she'll marry you? Maybe she feels the same way Mother does?

CHRIS: Well, if she does, then that's the end of it. From her letters I think she's forgotten him. I'll find out. And then we'll thrash it out with Mother? Right? Dad, don't avoid me.

KELLER: The trouble is, you don't see enough women. You never did.

CHRIS: So what? I'm not fast with women.

KELLER: I don't see why it has to be Annie.

CHRIS: Because it is.

KELLER: That's a good answer, but it don't answer anything. You haven't seen her since you went to war. It's five years.

CHRIS: I can't help it. I know her best. I was brought up next door to her. These years when I think of someone for my wife, I think of Annie. What do you want, a diagram?

KELLER: I don't want a diagram . . . I – I'm — She thinks he's coming back, Chris. You marry that girl and you're pronouncing him dead. Now what's going to happen to Mother? Do you know? I don't! (*Pause.*)

CHRIS: All right, then, Dad.

KELLER (*thinking Chris has retreated*): Give it some more thought.

CHRIS: I've given it three years of thought. I'd hoped that if I waited, Mother would forget Larry and then we'd have a regular wedding and everything happy. But if that can't happen here, then I'll have to get out.

KELLER: What the hell is *this?*

CHRIS: I'll get out. I'll get married and live some place else. Maybe in New York.

KELLER: Are you crazy?

CHRIS: I've been a good son too long, a good sucker. I'm through with it.

KELLER: You've got a business here, what the hell is this?

CHRIS: The business! The business doesn't inspire me.

KELLER: Must you be inspired?

CHRIS: Yes. I like it an hour a day. If I have to grub for money all day long at least at evening I want it beautiful. I want a family, I want some kids, I want to build something I can give myself to. Annie is in the middle of that. Now . . . where do I find it?

KELLER: You mean — (*Goes to him.*) Tell me something, you mean you'd leave the business?

CHRIS: Yes. On this I would.

KELLER (*after a pause*): Well . . . you don't want to think like that.

CHRIS: Then help me stay here.

KELLER: All right, but – but don't think like that. Because what the hell did I work for? That's only for you, Chris, the whole shootin' match is for you!

CHRIS: I know that, Dad. Just you help me stay here.

KELLER (*putting a fist up to Chris's jaw*): But don't think that way, you hear me?

CHRIS: I am thinking that way.

KELLER (*lowering his hand*): I don't understand you, do I?

CHRIS: No, you don't. I'm a pretty tough guy.

KELLER: Yeah. I can see that.

    MOTHER *appears on porch. She is in her early fifties, a woman of uncontrolled inspirations and an overwhelming capacity for love.*

MOTHER: Joe?

CHRIS (*going towards porch*): Hello, Mom.

MOTHER (*indicating house behind her; to Keller*): Did you take a bag from under the sink?

KELLER: Yeah, I put it in the pail.

MOTHER: Well, get it out of the pail. That's my potatoes.

    CHRIS *bursts out laughing – goes up into alley.*

KELLER (*laughing*): I thought it was garbage.

MOTHER: Will you do me a favour, Joe? Don't be helpful.

KELLER: I can afford another bag of potatoes.

MOTHER: Minnie scoured that pail in boiling water last night. It's cleaner than your teeth.

KELLER: And I don't understand why, after I worked forty years and I got a maid, why I have to take out the garbage.

MOTHER: If you would make up your mind that every bag in the kitchen isn't full of garbage you wouldn't be throwing out my vegetables. Last time it was the onions.

    CHRIS *comes on, hands her bag.*

KELLER: I don't like garbage in the house.

MOTHER: Then don't eat. (*She goes into the kitchen with bag.*)

CHRIS: That settles you for today.

KELLER: Yeah, I'm in last place again. I don't know, once upon a time I used to think that when I got money again I would have a maid and my wife would take it easy. Now I got money, and I got a maid, and my wife is workin' for the maid. (*He sits in one of the chairs.*)

MOTHER *comes out on last line. She carries a pot of string beans.*

MOTHER: It's her day off, what are you crabbing about?

CHRIS (*to Mother*): Isn't Annie finished eating?

MOTHER (*looking around preoccupiedly at yard*): She'll be right out. (*Moves.*) That wind did some job on this place. (*Of the tree*): So much for that, thank God.

KELLER (*indicating chair beside him*): Sit down, take it easy.

MOTHER (*pressing her hand to top of her head*): I've got such a funny pain on the top of my head.

CHRIS: Can I get you an aspirin?

MOTHER *picks a few petals off ground, stands there smelling them in her hand, then sprinkles them over plants.*

MOTHER: No more roses. It's so funny . . . everything decides to happen at the same time. This month is his birthday; his tree blows down, Annie comes. Everything that happened seems to be coming back. I was just down the cellar, and what do I stumble over? His baseball glove. I haven't seen it in a century.

CHRIS: Don't you think Annie looks well?

MOTHER: Fine. There's no question about it. She's a beauty . . . I still don't know what brought her here. Not that I'm not glad to see her, but —

CHRIS: I just thought we'd all like to see each other again. (MOTHER *just looks at him, nodding ever so slightly – almost as though admitting something.*) And I wanted to see her myself.

MOTHER (*as her nods halt, to Keller*): The only thing is I think her nose got longer. But I'll always love that girl. She's one that didn't jump into bed with somebody else as soon as it happened with her fella.

KELLER (*as though that were impossible for Annie*): Oh, what're you —?

MOTHER: Never mind. Most of them didn't wait till the telegrams were opened. I'm just glad she came, so you can see I'm not *completely* out of my mind. (*Sits, and rapidly breaks string beans in the pot.*)

CHRIS: Just because she isn't married doesn't mean she's been mourning Larry.

MOTHER (*with an undercurrent of observation*): Why then isn't she?

CHRIS (*a little flustered*): Well . . . it could've been any number of things.

MOTHER (*directly at him*): Like what, for instance?

CHRIS (*embarrassed, but standing his ground*): I don't know. Whatever it is. Can I get you an aspirin?

　　MOTHER *puts her hand to her head. She gets up and goes aimlessly towards the trees on rising.*

MOTHER: It's not like a headache.

KELLER: You don't sleep, that's why. She's wearing out more bedroom slippers than shoes.

MOTHER: I had a terrible night. (*She stops moving.*) I never had a night like that.

CHRIS (*looking at Keller*): What was it, Mom? Did you dream?

MOTHER: More, more than a dream.

CHRIS (*hesitantly*): About Larry?

MOTHER: I was fast asleep, and — (*Raising her arm over the audience.*) Remember the way he used to fly low past the house when he was in training? When we used to see his face in the cockpit going by? That's the way I saw him. Only high up. Way, way up, where the clouds are. He was so real I could reach out and touch him. And suddenly he started to fall. And crying, crying to me . . . Mom, Mom! I could hear him like he was in the room. Mom! . . . it was his voice! If I could touch him I knew I could stop him, if I could only – (*Breaks off, allowing her outstretched hand to fall.*) I woke up and it was so funny – The wind . . . it was like the roaring of his engine. I came out here . . . I must've still been half asleep. I could hear that roaring like he was going by. The tree snapped right in front of me – and I like – came awake. (*She is looking at tree. She suddenly realizes something, turns with a reprimanding finger shaking slightly at Keller.*) See? We should never have planted that tree. I said so in the first place; it was too soon to plant a tree for him.

CHRIS (*alarmed*): Too soon!

MOTHER (*angering*): We rushed into it. Everybody was in such a hurry to bury him. I *said* not to plant it yet. (*To Keller.*) I *told* you to —!

CHRIS: Mother, Mother! (*She looks into his face.*) The wind blew it down. What significance has that got? What are you talking about? Mother, please ... Don't go through it all again, will you? It's no good, it doesn't accomplish anything. I've been thinking, y'know? – maybe we ought to put our minds to forgetting him?

MOTHER: That's the third time you've said that this week.

CHRIS: Because it's not right; we never took up our lives again. We're like at a railroad station waiting for a train that never comes in.

MOTHER (*pressing top of her head*): Get me an aspirin, heh?

CHRIS: Sure, and let's break out of this, heh, Mom? I thought the four of us might go out to dinner a couple of nights, maybe go dancing out at the shore.

MOTHER: Fine. (*To Keller.*) We can do it tonight.

KELLER: Swell with me!

CHRIS: Sure, let's have some fun. (*To Mother.*) You'll start with this aspirin. (*He goes up and into house with new spirit. Her smile vanishes.*)

MOTHER (*with an accusing undertone*): Why did he invite her here?

KELLER: Why does that bother you?

MOTHER: She's been in New York three and a half years, why all of a sudden —?

KELLER: Well, maybe – maybe he just wanted to see her.

MOTHER: Nobody comes seven hundred miles 'just to see'.

KELLER: What do you mean? He lived next door to the girl all his life, why shouldn't he want to see her again? (MOTHER *looks at him critically*.) Don't look at me like that, he didn't tell me any more than he told you.

MOTHER (*a warning and a question*): He's not going to marry her.

KELLER: How do you know he's even thinking of it?

MOTHER: It's got that about it.

KELLER (*sharply watching her reaction*): Well? So what?

MOTHER (*alarmed*): What's going on here, Joe?

KELLER: Now listen, kid —

MOTHER (*avoiding contact with him*): She's not his girl, Joe; she knows she's not.

KELLER: You can't read her mind.

MOTHER: Then why is she still single? New York is full of men, why isn't she married? (*Pause.*) Probably a hundred people told her she's foolish, but she's waited.

KELLER: How do you know why she waited?

MOTHER: She knows what I know, that's why. She's faithful as a rock. In my worst moments, I think of her waiting, and I know again that I'm right.

KELLER: Look, it's a nice day. What are we arguing for?

MOTHER (*warningly*): Nobody in this house dast take her faith away, Joe. Strangers might. But not his father, not his brother.

KELLER (*exasperated*): What do you want me to do? What do you want?

MOTHER: I want you to act like he's coming back. Both of you. Don't think I haven't noticed you since Chris invited her. I won't stand for any nonsense.

KELLER: But, Kate —

MOTHER: Because if he's not coming back, then I'll kill myself! Laugh. Laugh at me. (*She points to tree.*) But why did that happen the very night she came back? Laugh, but there are meanings in such things. She goes to sleep in his room and his memorial breaks in pieces. Look at it; look. (*She sits on bench.*) Joe —

KELLER: Calm yourself.

MOTHER: Believe with me, Joe. I can't stand all alone.

KELLER: Calm yourself.

MOTHER: Only last week a man turned up in Detroit, missing longer than Larry. You read it yourself.

KELLER: All right, all right, calm yourself.

MOTHER: You above all have got to believe, you —

KELLER (*rising*): Why me above all?

MOTHER: Just don't stop believing.

KELLER: What does that mean, me above all?

> BERT *comes rushing on.*

BERT: Mr Keller! Say, Mr Keller . . . (*Pointing up driveway.*) Tommy just said it again!

KELLER (*not remembering any of it*): Said what? Who?

BERT: The dirty word.

KELLER: Oh. Well —

BERT: Gee, aren't you going to arrest him? I warned him.

MOTHER (*with suddenness*): Stop that, Bert. Go home. (BERT *backs up, as she advances.*) There's no jail here.

KELLER (*as though to say, 'Oh-what-the-hell-let-him-believe-there-is'*): Kate —

MOTHER (*turning on Keller furiously*): There's no jail here! I want you to stop that jail business! (*He turns, shamed, but peeved.*)

BERT (*past her to Keller*): He's right across the street.

MOTHER: Go home, Bert. (BERT *turns around and goes up driveway. She is shaken. Her speech is bitten off, extremely urgent.*) I want you to stop that, Joe. That whole jail business!

KELLER (*alarmed, therefore angered*): Look at you, look at you shaking.

MOTHER (*trying to control herself, moving about clasping her hands*): I can't help it.

KELLER: What have I got to hide? What the hell is the matter with you Kate?

MOTHER: I didn't say you had anything to hide, I'm just telling you to stop it! Now stop it! (*As ANN and CHRIS appear on porch. ANN is twenty-six, gentle but despite herself capable of holding fast to what she knows. CHRIS opens door for her.*)

ANN: Hya, Joe! (*She leads off a general laugh that is not self-conscious because they know one another too well.*)

CHRIS (*bringing Ann down, with an outstretched, chivalric arm*): Take a breath of that air, kid. You never get air like that in New York.

MOTHER (*genuinely overcome with it*): Annie, where did you get that dress!

ANN: I couldn't resist. I'm taking it right off before I ruin it. (*Swings around.*) How's that for three weeks' salary?

MOTHER (*to Keller*): Isn't she the most —? (*To Ann.*) It's gorgeous, simply gor —

CHRIS (*to Mother*): No kidding, now, isn't she the prettiest gal you ever saw?

MOTHER (*caught short by his obvious admiration, she finds herself reaching out for a glass of water and aspirin in his hand, and —*): You gained a little weight, didn't you, darling? (*She gulps pill and drinks.*)

ANN: It comes and goes.

KELLER: Look how nice her legs turned out!

ANN (*as she runs to fence*): Boy, the poplars got thick, didn't they?

    KELLER *moves to settee and sits.*

KELLER: Well, it's three years, Annie. We're gettin' old, kid.

MOTHER: How does Mom like New York? (ANN *keeps looking through trees.*)

ANN (*a little hurt*): Why'd they take our hammock away?

KELLER: Oh, no, it broke. Couple of years ago.

MOTHER: What broke? He had one of his light lunches and flopped into it.

ANN (*laughs and turns back towards Jim's yard*): Oh, excuse me!

    JIM *has come to fence and is looking over it. He is smoking a cigar. As she cries out, he comes on around on stage.*

JIM: How do you do. (*To Chris.*) She looks very intelligent!

CHRIS: Ann, this is Jim – Doctor Bayliss.

ANN (*shaking Jim's hand*): Oh, sure, he writes a lot about you.

JIM: Don't you believe it. He likes everybody. In the battalion he was known as Mother McKeller.

ANN: I can believe it. You know —? (*To Mother.*) It's so strange seeing him come out of that yard. (*To Chris.*) I guess I never grew up. It almost seems that Mom and Pop are in there now. And you and my brother doing algebra, and Larry trying to copy my home-work. Gosh, those dear dead days beyond recall.

JIM: Well, I hope that doesn't mean you want me to move out?

SUE (*calling from offstage*): Jim, come in here! Mr Hubbard is on the phone!

JIM: I told you I don't want —

SUE (*commandingly sweet*): Please, dear! Please!

JIM (*resigned*): All right, Susie. (*Trailing off.*) All right, all right ... (*To Ann.*) I've only met you, Ann, but if I may offer you a piece of advice – When you marry, never – even in your mind – never count your husband's money.

SUE (*from offstage*): Jim?

JIM: At once! (*Turns and goes off.*) At once. (*He exits.*)

MOTHER (ANN *is looking at her. She speaks meaningfully*): I told her to take up the guitar. It'd be a common interest for them. (*They laugh.*) Well, he loves the guitar!

ANN, *as though to overcome Mother, becomes suddenly lively, crosses to Keller on settee, sits on his lap.*

ANN: Let's eat at the shore tonight! Raise some hell around here, like we used to before Larry went!

MOTHER (*emotionally*): You think of him! You see? (*Triumphantly.*) She thinks of him!

ANN (*with an uncomprehending smile*): What do you mean, Kate?

MOTHER: Nothing. Just that you – remember him, he's in your thoughts.

ANN: That's a funny thing to say; how could I help remembering him?

MOTHER (*it is drawing to a head the wrong way for her; she starts anew. She rises and comes to Ann*): Did you hang up your things?

ANN: Yeah ... (*To Chris.*) Say, you've sure gone in for clothes. I could hardly find room in the closet.

MOTHER: No, don't you remember? That's Larry's room.

ANN: You mean ... they're Larry's?

MOTHER: Didn't you recognize them?

ANN (*slowly rising, a little embarrassed*): Well, it never occurred to me that you'd – I mean the shoes are all shined.

MOTHER: Yes, dear. (*Slight pause,* ANN *can't stop staring at her.* MOTHER *breaks it by speaking with the relish of gossip, putting her arm around Ann and walking with her.*) For so long I've been aching for a nice conversation with you, Annie. Tell me something.

ANN: What?

MOTHER: I don't know. Something nice.

CHRIS (*wryly*): She means do you go out much?

MOTHER: Oh, shut up.

KELLER: And are any of them serious?

MOTHER (*laughing, sits in her chair*): Why don't you both choke?

KELLER: Annie, you can't go into a restaurant with that woman any more. In five minutes thirty-nine strange people are sitting at the table telling her their life story.

MOTHER: If I can't ask Annie a personal question —

KELLER: Askin' is all right, but don't beat her over the head. You're beatin' her, you're beatin' her. (*They are laughing.*)

ANN *takes pan of beans off stool, puts them on floor under chair and sits.*

ANN (*to Mother*): Don't let them bulldoze you. Ask me anything you like. What do you want to know, Kate? Come on, let's gossip.

MOTHER (*to Chris and Keller*): She's the only one is got any sense. (*To Ann.*) Your mother – she's not getting a divorce, heh?

ANN: No, she's calmed down about it now. I think when he gets out they'll probably live together. In New York, of course.

MOTHER: That's fine. Because your father is still – I mean he's a decent man after all is said and done.

ANN: I don't care. She can take him back if she likes.

MOTHER: And you? You – (*shakes her head negatively*) – go out much? (*Slight pause.*)

ANN (*delicately*): You mean am I still waiting for him?

MOTHER: Well, no. I don't expect you to wait for him but —

ANN (*kindly*): But that's what you mean, isn't it?

MOTHER: Well . . . yes.

ANN: Well, I'm not, Kate.

MOTHER (*faintly*): You're not?

ANN: Isn't it ridiculous? You don't really imagine he's —?

MOTHER: I know, dear, but don't say it's ridiculous, because the papers were full of it; I don't know about New York, but there was half a page about a man missing even longer than Larry, and he turned up from Burma.

CHRIS (*coming to Ann*): He couldn't have wanted to come home very badly, Mom.

MOTHER: Don't be so smart.

CHRIS: You can have a helluva time in Burma.

ANN (*rises and swings around in back of Chris*): So I've heard.

CHRIS: Mother, I'll bet you money that you're the only woman in the country who after three years is still —

MOTHER: You're sure?

CHRIS: Yes, I am.

MOTHER: Well, if you're sure then you're sure. (*She turns her head away an instant.*) They don't say it on the radio but I'm sure that in the dark at night they're still waiting for their sons.

CHRIS: Mother, you're absolutely —

MOTHER (*waving him off*): Don't be so damned smart! Now stop it! (*Slight pause.*) There are just a few things you *don't* know. All of you. And I'll tell you one of them. Annie. Deep, deep in your heart you've always been waiting for him.

ANN (*resolutely*): No, Kate.

MOTHER (*with increasing demand*): But deep in your heart, Annie!

CHRIS: She ought to know, shouldn't she?

MOTHER: Don't let them tell you what to think. Listen to your heart. Only your heart.

ANN: Why does your heart tell you he's alive?

MOTHER: Because he has to be.

ANN: But why, Kate?

MOTHER (*going to her*): Because certain things have to be, and certain things can never be. Like the sun has to rise, it has to be. That's why there's God. Otherwise anything could happen. But there's God, so certain things can never happen. I would know, Annie – just like I knew the day he – (*indicates Chris*) – went into that terrible battle. Did he write me? Was it in the papers? No, but that morning I couldn't raise my head off the pillow. Ask Joe. Suddenly, I knew. I knew! And he was nearly killed that day. Ann, you *know* I'm right!

   ANN *stands there in silence, then turns trembling, going upstage.*

ANN: No, Kate.

MOTHER: I have to have some tea.

   FRANK *appears, carrying ladder.*

FRANK: Annie! (*Coming down.*) How are you, gee whiz!

ANN (*taking his hand*): Why, Frank, you're losing your hair.

KELLER: He's got responsibility.

FRANK: Gee whiz!

KELLER: Without Frank the stars wouldn't know when to come out.

FRANK (*laughs; to Ann*): You look more womanly. You've matured. You —

KELLER: Take it easy, Frank, you're a married man.

ANN (*as they laugh*): You still haberdashering?

FRANK: Why not? Maybe I too can get to be president. How's your brother? Got his degree, I hear.

ANN: Oh, George has his own office now!

FRANK: Don't say! (*Funereally.*) And your dad? Is he —?

ANN (*abruptly*): Fine. I'll be in to see Lydia.

FRANK (*sympathetically*): How about it, does Dad expect a parole soon?

ANN (*with growing ill-ease*): I really don't know, I —

FRANK (*staunchly defending her father for her sake*): I mean because I feel, y'know, that if an intelligent man like your father is put in prison, there ought to be a law that says either you execute him, or let him go after a year.

CHRIS (*interrupting*): Want a hand with that ladder, Frank?

FRANK (*taking cue*): That's all right, I'll —(*Picks up ladder.*) I'll finish the horoscope tonight, Kate. (*Embarrassed.*) See you later, Ann, you look wonderful. (*He exits. They look at Ann.*)

ANN (*to Chris, as she sits slowly on stool*): Haven't they stopped talking about Dad?

CHRIS (*comes down and sits on arm of chair*): Nobody talks about him any more.

KELLER (*rises and comes to her*): Gone and forgotten. kid.

ANN: Tell me. Because I don't want to meet anybody on the block if they're going to —

CHRIS: I don't want you to worry about it.

ANN (*to Keller*): Do they still remember the case, Joe? Do they talk about you?

KELLER: The only one still talks about it is my wife.

MOTHER: That's because you keep on playing policeman with the kids. All their parents hear out of you is jail, jail, jail.

KELLER: Actually what happened was that when I got home from the penitentiary the kids got very interested in me. You know kids. I was – (*laughs*) – like the expert on the jail situation. And as time passed they got it confused and . . . I ended up a detective. (*Laughs.*)

MOTHER: Except that *they* didn't get it confused. (*To Ann.*) He hands out police badges from the Post Toasties boxes. (*They laugh.*)

ANN *rises and comes to Keller, putting her arm around his shoulder.*

ANN (*wondrously at them, happy*): Gosh, it's wonderful to hear you laughing about it.

CHRIS: Why, what'd you expect?

ANN: The last thing I remember on this block was one word – 'Murderers!' Remember that, Kate? – Mrs Hammond standing in front of our house and yelling that word? She's still around, I suppose?

MOTHER: They're all still around.

KELLER: Don't listen to her. Every Saturday night the whole gang is playin' poker in this arbour. All the ones who yelled murderer takin' my money now.

MOTHER: Don't, Joe; she's a sensitive girl, don't fool her. (*To Ann.*) They still remember about Dad. It's different with him. (*Indicates Joe.*) He was exonerated, your father's still there. That's why I wasn't so enthusiastic about your coming. Honestly, I know how sensitive you are, and I told Chris, I said —-

KELLER: Listen, you do like I did and you'll be all right. The day I come home, I got out of my car – but not in front of the house . . . on the corner. You should've been here, Annie, and you too, Chris; you'd-a seen something. Everybody knew I was getting out that day; the porches were loaded. Picture it now; none of them believed I was innocent. The story was, I pulled a fast one getting myself exonerated. So I get out of my car, and I walk down the street. But very slow. And with a smile. The beast! I was the beast; the guy who sold cracked cylinder heads to the Army Air Force; the guy who made twenty-one P-40s crash in Australia. Kid, walkin' down the street that day I was guilty as hell. Except I wasn't, and there was a court paper in my pocket to prove I wasn't, and I walked . . . past . . . the porches. Result? Fourteen months later I had one of the best shops in the state again, a respected man again; bigger than ever.

CHRIS (*with admiration*): Joe McGuts.

KELLER (*now with great force*): That's the only way you lick 'em is guts! (*To Ann.*) The worst thing you did was to move away from here. You made it tough for your father when he gets out. That's why I tell you, I like to see him move back right on this block.

MOTHER (*pained*): How could they move back?

KELLER: It ain't gonna end *till* they move back! (*To Ann.*) Till people play cards with him again, and talk with him, and smile with him – you play cards with a man you know he can't be a murderer. And the next time you write him I like you to tell him just what I said. (ANN *simply stares at him.*) You hear me?

ANN (*surprised*): Don't you hold anything against him?

KELLER: Annie, I never believed in crucifying people.

ANN (*mystified*): But he was your partner, he dragged you through the mud.

KELLER: Well, he ain't my sweetheart, but you gotta forgive, don't you?

ANN: You, either, Kate? Don't you feel any —?

KELLER (*to Ann*): The next time you write Dad —

ANN: I don't write him.

KELLER (*struck*): Well, every now and then you —

ANN (*a little shamed, but determined*): No, I've *never* written to him. Neither has my brother. (*To Chris.*) Say, do you feel this way, too?

CHRIS: He murdered twenty-one pilots.

KELLER: What the hell kinda talk is that?

MOTHER: That's not a thing to say about a man.

ANN: What else can you say? When they took him away I followed him, went to him every visiting day. I was crying all the time. Until the news came about Larry. Then I realized. It's wrong to pity a man like that. Father or no father, there's only one way to look at him. He knowingly shipped out parts that would crash an airplane. And how do you know Larry wasn't one of them?

MOTHER: I was waiting for that. (*Going to her.*) As long as you're here, Annie, I want to ask you never to say that again.

ANN: You surprise me. I thought you'd be mad at him.

MOTHER: What your father did had nothing to do with Larry. Nothing.

ANN: But we can't know that.

MOTHER (*striving for control*): As long as you're here!

ANN (*perplexed*): But Kate —

MOTHER: Put that out of your head!

KELLER: Because —

MOTHER (*quickly to Keller*): That's all, that's enough. (*Places her hand on her head.*) Come inside now, and have some tea with me. (*She turns and goes up steps.*)

KELLER (*to Ann*): The one thing you —

MOTHER (*sharply*): He's not dead, so there's no argument! Now come!

KELLER (*angrily*): In a minute! (*Mother turns and goes into house.*) Now look Annie —

CHRIS: All right, Dad, forget it.

KELLER: No, she dasn't feel that way. Annie —

CHRIS: I'm sick of the whole subject, now cut it out.

KELLER: You want her to go on like this? (*To Ann.*) Those cylinder heads went into P-40s only. What's the matter with you? You know Larry never flew a P-40.

CHRIS: So who flew those P-40s, pigs?

KELLER: The man was a fool, but don't make a murderer out of him. You got no sense? Look what it does to her! (*To Ann.*) Listen, you gotta appreciate what was doin' in that shop in the war. The both of you! It was a madhouse. Every half hour the Major callin' for cylinder heads, they were whippin' us with the telephone. The trucks were hauling them away hot, damn near. I mean just try to see it human, see it human. All of a sudden a batch comes out with a crack. That happens, that's the business. A fine, hairline crack. All right, so – so he's a little man, your father, always scared of loud voices. What'll the Major say? — Half a day's production shot. . . . What'll I say? You know what I mean? Human. (*He pauses.*) So he takes out his tools and he – covers over the cracks. All right – that's bad, it's wrong, but that's what a little man does. If I could have gone in that day I'd a told him – junk 'em, Steve, we can afford it. But alone he was afraid. But I know he meant no harm. He believed they'd hold up a hundred per cent. That's a mistake, but it ain't murder. You mustn't feel that way about him. You understand me? It ain't right.

ANN (*she regards him a moment*): Joe, let's forget it.

KELLER: Annie, the day the news came about Larry he was in the next cell to mine – Dad. And he cried, Annie – he cried half the night.

ANN (*touched*): He shoulda cried all night. (*Slight pause.*)

KELLER (*almost angered*): Annie, I do not understand why you —!

CHRIS (*breaking in – with nervous urgency*): Are you going to stop it?

ANN: Don't yell at him. He just wants everybody happy.

KELLER (*clasps her around waist, smiling*): That's my sentiments. Can you stand steak?

CHRIS: And champagne!

KELLER: Now you're operatin'! I'll call Swanson's for a table! Big time tonight, Annie!

ANN: Can't scare me.

KELLER (*to Chris, pointing at Ann*): I like that girl. Wrap her up. (*They laugh. Goes up porch.*) You got nice legs, Annie! ... I want to see everybody drunk tonight. (*Pointing to Chris.*) Look at him, he's blushin'! (*He exits, laughing, into house.*)

CHRIS (*calling after him*): Drink your tea, Casanova. (*He turns to Ann.*) Isn't he a great guy?

ANN: You're the only one I know who loves his parents.

CHRIS: I know. It went out of style, didn't it?

ANN (*with a sudden touch of sadness*): It's all right. It's a good thing. (*She looks about.*) You know? It's lovely here. The air is sweet.

CHRIS (*hopefully*): You're not sorry you came?

ANN: Not sorry, no. But I'm – not going to stay.

CHRIS: Why?

ANN: In the first place, your mother as much as told me to go.

CHRIS: Well —

ANN: You saw that – and then you – you've been kind of —

CHRIS: What?

ANN: Well . . . kind of embarrassed ever since I got here.

CHRIS: The trouble is I planned on kind of sneaking up on you over a period of a week or so. But they take it for granted that we're all set.

ANN: I knew they would. Your mother anyway.

CHRIS: How did you know?

ANN: From *her* point of view, why else would I come?

CHRIS: Well . . . would you want to? (ANN *still studies him.*) I guess you know this is why I asked you to come.

ANN: I guess this is why I came.

CHRIS: Ann, I love you. I love you a great deal. (*Finally.*) I love you. (*Pause. She waits.*) I have no imagination . . . that's all I know to tell you. (ANN *is waiting, ready.*) I'm embarrassing you. I didn't want to tell it to you here. I wanted some place we'd never been; a place where we'd be brand new to each other. . . . You feel it's wrong here, don't you? This yard, this chair? I want you to be ready for me. I don't want to win you away from anything.

ANN (*putting her arms around him*): Oh, Chris, I've been ready a long, long time!

CHRIS: Then he's gone forever. You're sure.

ANN: I almost got married two years ago.

CHRIS: Why didn't you?

ANN: You started to write to me — (*Slight pause.*)

CHRIS: You felt something that far back?

ANN: Every day since!

CHRIS: Ann, why didn't you let me know?

ANN: I was waiting for you, Chris. Till then you never wrote, And when you did, what did you say? You sure can be ambiguous, you know.

CHRIS (*looks towards house, then at her, trembling*): Give me a kiss,

Ann. Give me a — (*They kiss.*) God, I kissed you, Annie, I kissed Annie. How long, how long I've been waiting to kiss you!

ANN: I'll never forgive you. Why did you wait all these years? All I've done is sit and wonder if I was crazy for thinking of you.

CHRIS: Annie, we're going to live now! I'm going to make you so happy. (*He kisses her, but without their bodies touching.*)

ANN (*a little embarrassed*): Not like that you're not.

CHRIS: I kissed you . . .

ANN: Like Larry's brother. Do it like you, Chris. (*He breaks away from her abruptly.*) What is it, Chris?

CHRIS: Let's drive some place . . . I want to be alone with you.

ANN: No . . . what is it, Chris, your mother?

CHRIS: No – nothing like that.

ANN: Then what's wrong? Even in your letters, there was something ashamed.

CHRIS: Yes, I suppose I have been. But it's going from me.

ANN: You've got to tell me —

CHRIS: I don't know how to start. (*He takes her hand.*)

ANN: It wouldn't work this way. (*Slight pause.*)

CHRIS (*speaks quietly, factually at first*): It's all mixed up with so many other things. . . . You remember, overseas, I was in command of a company?

ANN: Yeah, sure.

CHRIS: Well, I lost them.

ANN: How many?

CHRIS: Just about all.

ANN: Oh, gee!

CHRIS: It takes a little time to toss that off. Because they weren't just men. For instance, one time it'd been raining several days and this kid came to me, and gave me his last pair of dry socks. Put them in my pocket. That's only a little thing – but . . . that's the kind of guys I had. They didn't die; they killed themselves for each other. I mean that exactly; a little more selfish and they'd 've been here today. And I got an idea – watching them go down. Everything was being destroyed, see, but it seemed to me that one new thing was made. A kind of – responsibility. Man for man. You understand me? – To show that, to bring that on to the earth again like some kind of a monument and everyone would feel it standing there, behind him, and it would make a difference to him. (*Pause.*) And then I came home and it was incredible. I – there was no meaning in it here; the whole thing to them was a kind of a – bus accident. I went to work with Dad, and that rat-race again. I felt – what you said – ashamed somehow. Because nobody was changed at all. It seemed to make suckers out of a lot of guys. I felt wrong to be alive, to open the bank-book, to drive the new car, to see the new refrigerator. I mean you can take those things out of a war, but when you drive that car you've got to know that it came out of the love a man can have for a man, you've got to be a little better because of that. Otherwise what you have is really loot, and there's blood on it. I didn't want to take any of it. And I guess that included you.

ANN: And you still feel that way?

CHRIS: I want you now, Annie.

ANN: Because you mustn't feel that way any more. Because you have a right to whatever you have. Everything, Chris, understand that? To me, too ... And the money, there's nothing wrong in your money. Your father put hundreds of planes in the air, you should be proud. A man should be paid for that ...

CHRIS: Oh Annie, Annie ... I'm going to make a fortune for you!

KELLER (*offstage*): Hello ... Yes. Sure.

ANN (*laughing softly*): What'll I do with a fortune?

    They kiss. KELLER *enters from house.*

KELLER (*thumbing towards house*): Hey, Ann, your brother — (*They step apart shyly.* KELLER *comes down, and wryly.*) What is this, Labour Day?

CHRIS (*waving him away, knowing the kidding will be endless*): All right, all right.

ANN: You shouldn't burst out like that.

KELLER: Well, nobody told me it was Labour Day. (*Looks around.*) Where's the hot dogs?

CHRIS (*loving it*): All right. You said it once.

KELLER: Well, as long as I know it's Labour Day from now on, I'll wear a bell around my neck.

ANN (*affectionately*): He's so subtle!

CHRIS: George Bernard Shaw as an elephant.

KELLER: George! – hey, you kissed it out of my head – your brother's on the phone.

ANN (*surprised*): My brother?

KELLER: Yeah, George. Long distance.

ANN: What's the matter, is anything wrong?

KELLER: I don't know, Kate's talking to him. Hurry up, she'll cost him five dollars.

ANN (*takes a step upstage, then comes down towards Chris*): I wonder if we ought to tell your mother yet? I mean I'm not very good in an argument.

CHRIS: We'll wait till tonight. After dinner. Now don't get tense, just leave it to me.

KELLER: What're you telling her?

CHRIS: Go ahead, Ann. (*With misgivings, ANN goes up and into house.*) We're getting married, Dad. (KELLER *nods indecisively.*) Well, don't you say anything?

KELLER (*distracted*): I'm glad, Chris, I'm just – George is calling from Columbus.

CHRIS: Columbus!

KELLER: Did Annie tell you he was going to see his father today?

CHRIS: No, I don't think she knew anything about it.

KELLER (*asking uncomfortably*): Chris! You – you think you know her pretty good?

CHRIS (*hurt and apprehensive*): What kind of a question?

KELLER: I'm just wondering. All these years George don't go to
see his father. Suddenly he goes . . . and she comes here.

CHRIS: Well, what about it?

KELLER: It's crazy, but it comes to my mind. She don't hold
nothin' against me, does she?

CHRIS (*angry*): I don't know what you're talking about.

KELLER (*a little more combatively*): I'm just talkin'. To his last day
in court the man blamed it all on me; and this is his daughter.
I mean if she was sent here to find out something?

CHRIS (*angered*): Why? What is there to find out?

ANN (*on phone, offstage*): Why are you so excited, George? What
happened there?

KELLER: I mean if they want to open up the case again, for the
nuisance value, to hurt us?

CHRIS: Dad . . . how could you think that of her?

ANN (*still on phone*): But what did he say to you, for
God's sake? } *Together*

KELLER: It couldn't be, heh. You know.

CHRIS: Dad, you amaze me . . .

KELLER (*breaking in*): All right, forget it, forget it. (*With great
force, moving about.*) I want a clean start for you, Chris. I want a
new sign over the plant – Christopher Keller, Incorporated.

CHRIS (*a little uneasily*): J. O. Keller is good enough.

KELLER: We'll talk about it. I'm going to build you a house,
stone, with a driveway from the road. I want you to spread out,
Chris, I want you to use what I made for you. (*He is close to him
now.*) I mean, with joy, Chris, without shame . . . with joy.

CHRIS (*touched*): I will, Dad.

KELLER (*with deep emotion*): Say it to me.

CHRIS: Why?

KELLER: Because sometimes I think you're . . . ashamed of the
money.

CHRIS: No, don't feel that.

KELLER: Because it's good money, there's nothing wrong with
that money.

CHRIS (*a little frightened*): Dad, you don't have to tell me this.

KELLER (*with overriding affection and self-confidence now. He grips Chris by the back of the neck, and with laughter between his determined jaws*): Look, Chris, I'll go to work on Mother for you. We'll get her so drunk tonight we'll all get married! (*Steps away, with a wide gesture of his arm.*) There's gonna be a wedding, kid, like there never was seen! Champagne, tuxedos —!

He breaks off as ANN's *voice comes out loud from the house where she is still talking on phone.*

ANN: Simply because when you get excited you don't control yourself. . . . (*Mother comes out of house.*) Well, what did he tell you for God's sake? (*Pause.*) All right, come then. (*Pause.*) Yes, they'll all be here. Nobody's running away from you. And try to get hold of yourself, will you? (*Pause.*) All right, all right. Good-bye.

There is a brief pause as ANN *hangs up receiver, then comes out of kitchen.*

CHRIS: Something happen?

KELLER: He's coming here?

ANN: On the seven o'clock. He's in Columbus. (*To Mother.*) I told him it would be all right.

KELLER: Sure, fine! Your father took sick?

ANN (*mystified*): No, George didn't say he was sick. I — (*Shaking it off.*) I don't know. I suppose it's something stupid, you know my brother — (*She comes to Chris.*) Let's go for a drive, or something . . .

CHRIS: Sure. Give me the keys, Dad.

MOTHER: Drive through the park. It's beautiful now.

CHRIS: Come on, Ann. (*To them.*) Be back right away.

ANN (*as she and* CHRIS *exit up driveway*): See you.

MOTHER *comes down towards Keller, her eyes fixed on him.*

KELLER: Take your time. (*To Mother.*) What does George want?

MOTHER: He's been in Columbus since this morning with Steve. He's gotta see Annie right away, he says.

KELLER: What for?

MOTHER: I don't know. (*She speaks with warnings.*) He's a lawyer now, Joe. George is a lawyer. All these years he never even sent a postcard to Steve. Since he got back from the war, not a postcard.

KELLER: So what?

MOTHER (*her tension breaking out*): Suddenly he takes an airplane from New York to see him. An airplane!

KELLER: Well? So?

MOTHER (*trembling*): Why?

KELLER: I don't read minds. Do you?

MOTHER: Why, Joe? What has Steve suddenly got to tell him that he takes an airplane to see him?

KELLER: What do I care what Steve's got to tell him?

MOTHER: You're sure, Joe?

KELLER (*frightened, but angry*): Yes, I'm sure.

MOTHER (*sits stiffly in a chair*): Be smart now, Joe. The boy is coming. Be smart.

KELLER (*desperately*): Once and for all, did you hear what I said? I said I'm sure!

MOTHER (*nods weakly*): All right, Joe. (*He straightens up.*) Just . . . be smart.

    KELLER, *in hopeless fury, looks at her, turns around, goes up to porch and into house, slamming screen door violently behind him.* MOTHER *sits in chair downstage, stiffly, staring, seeing.*

CURTAIN

ACT TWO

As twilight falls, that evening.

On the rise, CHRIS *is discovered sawing the broken-off tree, leaving stump standing alone. He is dressed in good pants, white shoes, but without a shirt. He disappears with tree up the alley when* MOTHER *appears on porch. She has on a dressing gown, carries a tray of grapejuice drink in a pitcher, and glasses with sprigs of mint in them.*

MOTHER (*calling up alley*): Did you have to put on good pants to do that? (*She comes downstage and puts tray on table in the arbour. Then looks around uneasily, then feels pitcher for coolness. Chris enters from alley brushing off his hands.*) You notice there's more light with that thing gone?

CHRIS: Why aren't you dressing?

MOTHER: It's suffocating upstairs. I made a grape drink for Georgie. He always liked grape. Come and have some.

CHRIS (*impatiently*): Well, come on, get dressed. And what's Dad sleeping so much for? (*He goes to table and pours a glass of juice.*)

MOTHER: He's worried. When he's worried he sleeps. (*Pauses. Looks into his eyes.*) We're dumb, Chris. Dad and I are stupid people. We don't know anything. You've got to protect us.

CHRIS: You're silly; what's there to be afraid of?

MOTHER: To his last day in court Steve never gave up the idea that Dad made him do it. If they're going to open the case again I won't live through it.

CHRIS: George is just a damn fool, Mother. How can you take him seriously?

MOTHER: That family hates us. Maybe even Annie —

CHRIS: Oh, now, Mother . . .

MOTHER: You think just because you like everybody, they like you!

CHRIS: All right, stop working yourself up. Just leave everything to me.

MOTHER: When George goes home tell her to go with him.

CHRIS (*noncommittally*): Don't worry about Annie.

MOTHER: Steve is her father, too.

CHRIS: Are you going to cut it out? Now, come.

MOTHER (*going upstage with him*): You don't realize how people can hate, Chris, they can hate so much they'll tear the world to pieces.

ANN, *dressed up, appears on porch.*

CHRIS: Look! She's dressed already. (*As he and* MOTHER *mount porch.*) I've just got to put on a shirt.

ANN (*in a preoccupied way*): Are you feeling well, Kate?

MOTHER: What's the difference, dear? There are certain people, y'know, the sicker they get the longer they live. (*She goes into house.*)

CHRIS: You look nice.

ANN: We're going to tell her tonight.

CHRIS: Absolutely, don't worry about it.

ANN: I wish we could tell her now. I can't stand scheming. My stomach gets hard.

CHRIS: It's not scheming, we'll just get her in a better mood.

MOTHER (*offstage in the house*): Joe, are you going to sleep all day?

ANN (*laughing*): The only one who's relaxed is your father. He's fast asleep.

CHRIS: I'm relaxed.

ANN: Are you?

CHRIS: Look. (*He holds out his hand and makes it shake.*) Let me know when George gets here.

He goes into the house. ANN *moves aimlessly, and then is drawn towards tree stump. She goes to it, hesitantly touches broken top in the hush of her thoughts. Offstage* LYDIA *calls, 'Johnny! Come get your supper!'* SUE *enters, and halts, seeing Ann.*

SUE: Is my husband —?

ANN (*turns, startled*): Oh!

SUE: I'm terribly sorry.

ANN: It's all right, I – I'm a little silly about the dark.

SUE (*looks about*): It is getting dark.

ANN: Are you looking for your husband?

SUE: As usual. (*Laughs tiredly.*) He spends so much time here, they'll be charging him rent.

ANN: Nobody was dressed, so he drove over to the depot to pick up my brother.

SUE: Oh, your brother's in?

ANN: Yeah, they ought to be here any minute now. Will you have a cold drink?

SUE: I will, thanks. (ANN *goes to table and pours.*) My husband! Too hot to drive me to beach. Men are like little boys; for the neighbours they'll always cut the grass.

ANN: People like to do things for the Kellers. Been that way since I can remember.

SUE: It's amazing. I guess your brother's coming to give you away, heh?

ANN (*giving her drink*): I don't know. I suppose.

SUE: You must be all nerved up.

ANN: It's always a problem getting yourself married, isn't it?

SUE: That depends on your shape, of course. I don't see why you should have had a problem.

ANN: I've had chances —

SUE: I'll bet. It's romantic . . . it's very unusual to me, marrying the brother of your sweetheart.

ANN: I don't know. I think it's mostly that whenever I need somebody to tell me the truth I've always thought of Chris. When he tells you something you know it's so. He relaxes me.

SUE: And he's got money. That's important, you know.

ANN: It wouldn't matter to me.

SUE: You'd be surprised. It makes all the difference. I married an intern. On my salary. And that was bad, because as soon as a

woman supports a man he owes her something. You can never
owe somebody without resenting them. (ANN *laughs.*) That's
true, you know.

ANN: Underneath, I think the doctor is very devoted.

SUE: Oh, certainly. But it's bad when a man always sees the bars
in front of him. Jim thinks he's in jail all the time.

ANN: Oh . . .

SUE: That's why I've been intending to ask you a small favour,
Ann. It's something very important to me.

ANN: Certainly, if I can do it.

SUE: You can. When you take up housekeeping, try to find a
place away from here.

ANN: Are you fooling?

SUE: I'm very serious. My husband is unhappy with Chris
around.

ANN: How is that?

SUE: Jim's a successful doctor. But he's got an idea he'd like to do
medical research. Discover things. You see?

ANN: Well, isn't that good?

SUE: Research pays twenty-five dollars a week minus laundering
the hair shirt. You've got to give up your life to go into it.

ANN: How does Chris —

SUE (*with growing feeling*): Chris makes people want to be better
than it's possible to be. He does that to people.

ANN: Is that bad?

SUE: My husband has a family, dear. Every time he has a session
with Chris he feels as though he's compromising by not giving
up everything for research. As though Chris or anybody else
isn't compromising. It happens with Jim every couple of years.
He meets a man and makes a statue out of him.

ANN: Maybe he's right. I don't mean that Chris is a statue, but —

SUE: Now darling, you know he's not right.

ANN: I don't agree with you. Chris —

SUE: Let's face it, dear. Chris is working with his father, isn't he?
He's taking money out of that business every week in the year.

ANN: What of it?

SUE: You ask me what of it?

ANN: I certainly do. (*She seems about to burst out.*) You oughtn't cast aspersions like that, I'm surprised at you.

SUE: You're surprised at me!

ANN: He'd never take five cents out of that plant if there was anything wrong with it.

SUE: You know that.

ANN: I know it. I resent everything you've said.

SUE (*moving towards her*): You know what I resent, dear?

ANN: Please, I don't want to argue.

SUE: I resent living next door to the Holy Family. It makes me look like a bum, you understand?

ANN: I can't do anything about that.

SUE: Who is he to ruin a man's life? Everybody knows Joe pulled a fast one to get out of jail.

ANN: That's not true!

SUE: Then why don't you go out and talk to people? Go on, talk to them. There's not a person on the block who doesn't know the truth.

ANN: That's a lie. People come here all the time for cards and —

SUE: So what? They give him credit for being smart. I do, too, I've got nothing against Joe. But if Chris wants people to put on the hair shirt let him take off his broadcloth. He's driving my husband crazy with that phony idealism of his, and I'm at the end of my rope on it! (CHRIS *enters on porch, wearing shirt and tie now. She turns quickly, hearing. With a smile.*) Hello, darling. How's Mother?

CHRIS: I thought George came.

SUE: No, it was just us.

CHRIS (*coming down to them*): Susie, do me a favour, heh? Go up to Mother and see if you can calm her. She's all worked up.

SUE: She still doesn't know about you two?

CHRIS (*laughs a little*): Well, she senses it, I guess. You know my mother.

SUE (*going up to porch*): Oh, yeah, she's psychic.

CHRIS: Maybe there's something in the medicine chest.

SUE: I'll give her one of everything. (*On porch.*) Don't worry about Kate; couple of drinks, dance her around a little ... She'll love Ann. (*To Ann.*) Because you're the female version of him. (CHRIS *laughs.*) Don't be alarmed. I said version. (*She goes into house.*)

CHRIS: Interesting woman, isn't she?

ANN: Yeah, she's very interesting.

CHRIS: She's a great nurse, you know, she —

ANN (*in tension, but trying to control it*): Are you still doing that?

CHRIS (*sensing something wrong, but still smiling*): Doing what?

ANN: As soon as you get to know somebody you find a distinction for them. How do you know she's a great nurse?

CHRIS: What's the matter, Ann?

ANN: The woman hates you. She despises you!

CHRIS: Hey ... What's hit you?

ANN: Gee, Chris —

CHRIS: What happened here?

ANN: You never — Why didn't you tell me?

CHRIS: Tell you what?

ANN: She says they think Joe is guilty.

CHRIS: What difference does it make what they think?

ANN: I don't care what they think, I just don't understand why you took the trouble to deny it. You said it was all forgotten.

CHRIS: I didn't want you to feel there was anything wrong in you coming here, that's all. I know a lot of people think my father was guilty, and I assumed there might be some question in your mind.

ANN: But I never once said I suspected him.

CHRIS: Nobody says it.

ANN: Chris, I know how much you love him, but it could never —

CHRIS: Do you think I could forgive him if he'd done that thing?

ANN: I'm not here out of a blue sky, Chris. I turned my back on my father, if there's anything wrong here now —

CHRIS: I know that, Ann.

ANN: George is coming from Dad, and I don't think it's with a blessing.

CHRIS: He's welcome here. You've got nothing to fear from George.

ANN: Tell me that ... Just tell me that.

CHRIS: The man is innocent, Ann. Remember he was falsely accused once and it put him through hell. How would you behave if you were faced with the same thing again? Annie, believe me, there's nothing wrong for you here, believe me, kid.

ANN: All right, Chris, all right. (*They embrace as* KELLER *appears quietly on porch.* ANN *simply studies him.*)

KELLER: Every time I come out here it looks like Playland! (*They break and laugh in embarrassment.*)

CHRIS: I thought you were going to shave?

KELLER (*sitting on bench*): In a minute. I just woke up, I can't see nothin'.

ANN: You look shaved.

KELLER: Oh, no. (*Massages his jaw.*) Gotta be extra special tonight. Big night, Annie. So how's it feel to be a married woman?

ANN (*laughs*): I don't know, yet.

KELLER (*to Chris*): What's the matter, you slippin'? (*He takes a little box of apples from under the bench as they talk.*)

CHRIS: The great roué!

KELLER: What is that, roué?

CHRIS: It's French.

KELLER: Don't talk dirty. (*They laugh.*)

CHRIS (*to Ann*): You ever meet a bigger ignoramus?

KELLER: Well, somebody's got to make a living.

ANN (*as they laugh*): That's telling him.

KELLER: I don't know, everybody's gettin' so Goddam educated in this country, there'll be nobody to take away the garbage. (*They laugh.*) It's gettin' so the only dumb ones left are the bosses.

ANN: You're not so dumb, Joe.

KELLER: I know, but you go into our plant, for instance. I got so many lieutenants, majors and colonels that I'm ashamed to ask somebody to sweep the floor. I gotta be careful I'll insult somebody. No kiddin'. It's a tragedy: you stand on the street today and spit, you're gonna hit a college man.

CHRIS: Well, don't spit.

KELLER (*breaks apple in half, passing it to Ann and Chris*): I mean to say, it's comin' to a pass. (*He takes a breath.*) I been thinkin', Annie ... your brother, George. I been thinkin' about your brother George. When he comes I like you to *brooch* something to him.

CHRIS: Broach.

KELLER: What's the matter with brooch?

CHRIS (*smiling*): It's not English.

KELLER: When I went to night school it was brooch.

ANN (*laughing*): Well, in day school it's broach.

KELLER: Don't surround me, will you? Seriously, Ann ... You say he's not well. George, I been thinkin', why should he knock himself out in New York with that cut-throat competition, when I got so many friends here; I'm very friendly with some big lawyers in town. I could set George up here.

ANN: That's awfully nice of you, Joe.

KELLER: No, kid, it ain't nice of me. I want you to understand me. I'm thinking of Chris. (*Slight pause.*) See ... this is what I mean. You get older, you want to feel that you – accomplished something. My only accomplishment is my son. I ain't brainy. That's all I accomplished. Now, a year, eighteen months, your father'll be a free man. Who is he going to come to, Annie? His baby. You. He'll come, old, mad, into your house.

ANN: That can't matter any more, Joe.

KELLER: I don't want that to come between us. (*Gestures between Chris and himself.*)

ANN: I can only tell you that could never happen.

KELLER: You're in love now, Annie, but believe me, I'm older than you and I know – a daughter is a daughter, and a father is a father. And it could happen. (*He pauses.*) I like you and George to go to him in prison and tell him . . . 'Dad, Joe wants to bring you into the business when you get out.'

ANN (*surprised, even shocked*): You'd have him as a partner?

KELLER: No, no partner. A good job. (*Pause. He sees she is shocked, a little mystified. He gets up, speaks more nervously.*) I want him to know, Annie . . . while he's sitting there I want him to know that when he gets out he's got a place waitin' for him. It'll take his bitterness away. To know you got a place . . . it sweetens you.

ANN: Joe, you owe him nothing.

KELLER: I owe him a good kick in the teeth, but he's your father.

CHRIS: Then kick him in the teeth! I don't want him in the plant, so that's that! You understand? And besides, don't talk about him like that. People misunderstand you!

KELLER: And I don't understand why she has to crucify the man.

CHRIS: Well, it's her father, if she feels —

KELLER: No, no.

CHRIS (*almost angrily*): What's it to you? Why —?

KELLER (*a commanding outburst in high nervousness*): A father is a father! (*As though the outburst had revealed him, he looks about, wanting to retract it. His hand goes to his cheek.*) I better – I better shave. (*He turns and a smile is on his face. To Ann.*) I didn't mean to yell at you, Annie.

ANN: Let's forget the whole thing, Joe.

KELLER: Right. (*To Chris.*) She's likeable.

CHRIS (*a little peeved at the man's stupidity*): Shave, will you?

KELLER: Right again.

As he turns to porch LYDIA *comes hurrying from her house.*

LYDIA: I forgot all about it. (*Seeing Chris and Ann.*) Hya. (*To*

Joe.) I promised to fix Kate's hair for tonight. Did she comb it yet?

KELLER: Always a smile, hey, Lydia?

LYDIA: Sure, why not?

KELLER (*going up on porch*): Come on up and comb my Katie's hair. (LYDIA *goes up on porch.*) She's got a big night, make her beautiful.

LYDIA: I will.

KELLER (*holds door open for her and she goes into kitchen. To Chris and Ann*): Hey, that could be a song. (*He sings softly.*)

'Come on up and comb my Katie's hair . . .

Oh, come on up, 'cause she's my lady fair —'

(*To Ann.*) How's that for one year of night school? (*He continues singing as he goes into kitchen.*)

'Oh, come on up, come on up, and comb my
lady's hair —'

JIM BAYLISS *rounds corner of driveway, walking rapidly.* JIM *crosses to Chris, motions him and pulls him down excitedly.* KELLER *stands just inside kitchen door, watching them.*

CHRIS: What's the matter? Where is he?

JIM: Where's your mother?

CHRIS: Upstairs, dressing.

ANN (*crossing to them rapidly*): What happened to George?

JIM: I asked him to wait in the car. Listen to me now. Can you take some advice? (*They wait.*) Don't bring him in here.

ANN: Why?

JIM: Kate is in bad shape, you can't explode this in front of her.

ANN: Explode what?

JIM: You know why he's here, don't try to kid it away. There's blood in his eye; drive him somewhere and talk to him alone.

ANN *turns to go up drive, takes a couple of steps, sees Keller, and stops. He goes quietly on into house.*

CHRIS (*shaken, and therefore angered*): Don't be an old lady.

JIM: He's come to take her home. What does that mean? (*To*

Ann.) You know what that means. Fight it out with him some place else.

ANN (*comes back down toward Chris*): I'll drive . . . him somewhere.

CHRIS (*goes to her*): No.

JIM: Will you stop being an idiot?

CHRIS: Nobody's afraid of him here. Cut that out!

He starts for driveway, but is brought up short by GEORGE, *who enters there. George is Chris's age, but a paler man, now on the edge of his self-restraint. He speaks quietly, as though afraid to find himself screaming. An instant's hesitation and* CHRIS *steps up to him, hand extended, smiling.*

CHRIS: Helluva way to do; what're you sitting out there for?

GEORGE: Doctor said your mother isn't well, I —

CHRIS: So what? She'd want to see you, wouldn't she? We've been waiting for you all afternoon. (*He puts his hand on George's arm, but* GEORGE *pulls away, coming across towards Ann.*)

ANN (*touching his collar*): This is filthy, didn't you bring another shirt?

GEORGE *breaks away from her, and moves down, examining the yard. Door opens, and he turns rapidly, thinking it is Kate, but it's* SUE. *She looks at him; he turns away and moves to fence. He looks over it at his former home.* SUE *comes downstage.*

SUE (*annoyed*): How about the beach, Jim?

JIM: Oh, it's too hot to drive.

SUE: How'd you get to the station – Zeppelin?

CHRIS: This is Mrs Bayliss, George. (*Calling as* GEORGE *pays no attention, staring at house.*) George! (GEORGE *turns.*) Mrs Bayliss.

SUE: How do you do.

GEORGE (*removing his hat*): You're the people who bought our house, aren't you?

SUE: That's right. Come and see what we did with it before you leave.

GEORGE (*walks down and away from her*): I liked it the way it was.

SUE (*after a brief pause*): He's frank, isn't he?

JIM (*pulling her off*): See you later. . . . Take it easy, fella. (*They exit.*)

CHRIS (*calling after them*): Thanks for driving him! (*Turning to George.*) How about some grape juice? Mother made it especially for you.

GEORGE (*with forced appreciation*): Good old Kate, remembered my grape juice.

CHRIS: You drank enough of it in this house. How've you been, George? – Sit down.

GEORGE (*keeps moving*): It takes me a minute. (*Looking around.*) It seems impossible.

CHRIS: What?

GEORGE: I'm back here.

CHRIS: Say, you've gotten a little nervous, haven't you?

GEORGE: Yeah, towards the end of the day. What're you, big executive now?

CHRIS: Just kind of medium. How's the law?

GEORGE: I don't know. When I was studying in the hospital it seemed sensible, but outside there doesn't seem to be much of a law. The trees got thick, didn't they? (*Points to stump.*) What's that?

CHRIS: Blew down last night. We had it there for Larry. You know.

GEORGE: Why, afraid you'll forget him?

CHRIS (*starts for George*): Kind of a remark is that?

ANN (*breaking in, putting a restraining hand on Chris*): When did you start wearing a hat?

GEORGE (*discovers hat in his hand*): Today. From now on I decided to look like a lawyer, anyway. (*He holds it up to her.*) Don't you recognize it?

ANN: Why? Where —?

GEORGE: Your father's – He asked me to wear it.

ANN: How is he?

GEORGE: He got smaller.

ANN: Smaller?

GEORGE: Yeah, little. (*Holds out his hand to measure.*) He's a little man. That's what happens to suckers, you know. It's good I went to him in time – another year there'd be nothing left but his smell.

CHRIS: What's the matter, George, what's the trouble?

GEORGE: The trouble? The trouble is when you make suckers out of people once, you shouldn't try to do it twice.

CHRIS: What does that mean?

GEORGE (*to Ann*): You're not married yet, are you?

ANN: George, will you sit down and stop —?

GEORGE: Are you married yet?

ANN: No, I'm not married yet.

GEORGE: You're not going to marry him.

ANN: Why am I not going to marry him?

GEORGE: Because his father destroyed your family.

CHRIS: Now look, George . . .

GEORGE: Cut it short, Chris. Tell her to come home with me. Let's not argue, you know what I've got to say.

CHRIS: George, you don't want to be the voice of God, do you?

GEORGE: I'm —

CHRIS: That's been your trouble all your life, George, you dive into things. What kind of a statement is that to make? You're a big boy now.

GEORGE: I'm a big boy now.

CHRIS: Don't come bulling in here. If you've got something to say, be civilized about it.

GEORGE: Don't civilize me!

ANN: Shhh!

CHRIS (*ready to hit him*): Are you going to talk like a grown man or aren't you?

ANN (*quickly, to forestall an outburst*): Sit down, dear. Don't be angry, what's the matter? (*He allows her to seat him, looking at her.*) Now what happened? You kissed me when I left, now you —

GEORGE (*breathlessly*): My life turned upside down since then. I

couldn't go back to work when you left. I wanted to go to
Dad and tell him you were going to be married. It seemed
impossible not to tell him. He loved you so much. (*He pauses.*)
Annie – we did a terrible thing. We can never be forgiven.
Not even to send him a card at Christmas. I didn't see him
once since I got home from the war! Annie, you don't know
what was done to that man. You don't know what happened.

ANN (*afraid*): Of course I know.

GEORGE: You can't know, you wouldn't be here. Dad came to
work that day. The night foreman came to him and showed
him the cylinder heads . . . they were coming out of the process with defects. There was something wrong with the process. So Dad went directly to the phone and called here and
told Joe to come down right away. But the morning passed.
No sign of Joe. So Dad called again. By this time he had over
a hundred defectives. The Army was screaming for stuff and
Dad didn't have anything to ship. So Joe told him . . . on the
phone he told him to weld, cover up the cracks in any way he
could, and ship them out.

CHRIS: Are you through now?

GEORGE (*surging up at him*): I'm not through now! (*Back to Ann.*)
Dad was afraid. He wanted Joe there if he was going to do it.
But Joe can't come down . . . He's sick. Sick! He suddenly gets
the flu! Suddenly! But he promised to take responsibility. Do
you understand what I'm saying? On the telephone you can't
have responsibility! In court you can always deny a phone call
and that's exactly what he did. They knew he was a liar the first
time, but in the appeal they believed that rotten lie and now
Joe is a big shot and your father is the patsy. (*He gets up.*) Now
what're you going to do? Eat his food, sleep in his bed? Answer
me; what're you going to do?

CHRIS: What're you going to do, George?

GEORGE: He's too smart for me, I can't prove a phone call.

CHRIS: Then how dare you come in here with that rot?

ANN: George, the court —

GEORGE: The court didn't know your father! But you know him. You know in your heart Joe did it.

CHRIS (*whirling him around*): Lower your voice or I'll throw you out of here!

GEORGE: She knows. She knows.

CHRIS (*to Ann*): Get him out of here, Ann. Get him out of here.

ANN: George. I know everything you've said. Dad told that whole thing in court, and they —

GEORGE (*almost a scream*): The court did not know him, Annie!

ANN: Shhh! – But he'll say anything, George. You know how quick he can lie.

GEORGE (*turning to Chris, with deliberation*): I'll ask you something, and look me in the eye when you answer me.

CHRIS: I'll look you in the eye.

GEORGE: You know your father —

CHRIS: I know him well.

GEORGE: And he's the kind of boss to let a hundred and twenty-one cylinder heads be repaired and shipped out of his shop without even knowing about it?

CHRIS: He's that kind of boss.

GEORGE: And that's the same Joe Keller who never left his shop without first going around to see that all the lights were out.

CHRIS (*with growing anger*): The same Joe Keller.

GEORGE: The same man who knows how many minutes a day his workers spend in the toilet.

CHRIS: The same man.

GEORGE: And my father, that frightened mouse who'd never buy a shirt without somebody along – that man would dare do such a thing on his own?

CHRIS: On his own. And because he's a frightened mouse this is another thing he'd do – throw the blame on somebody else because he'd not man enough to take it himself. He tried it in court but it didn't work, but with a fool like you it works!

GEORGE: Oh, Chris, you're a liar to yourself!

ANN (*deeply shaken*): Don't talk like that!

CHRIS (*sits facing George*): Tell me, George. What happened? The court record was good enough for you all these years, why isn't it good now? Why did you believe it all these years?

GEORGE (*after a slight pause*): Because you believed it. . . . That's the truth, Chris. I believed everything, because I thought you did. But today I heard it from his mouth. From his mouth it's altogether different than the record. Anyone who knows him, and knows your father, will believe it from his mouth. Your Dad took everything we have. I can't beat that. But she's one item he's not going to grab. (*He turns to Ann.*) Get your things. Everything they have is covered with blood. You're not the kind of a girl who can live with that. Get your things.

CHRIS: Ann . . . you're not going to believe that, are you?

ANN (*goes to him*): You know it's not true, don't you?

GEORGE: How can he tell you? It's his father. (*To Chris.*) None of these things ever even cross your mind?

CHRIS: Yes, they crossed my mind. Anything can cross your mind!

GEORGE: *He knows*, Annie. He knows!

CHRIS: The voice of God!

GEORGE: Then why isn't your name on the business? Explain that to her!

CHRIS: What the hell has that got to do with —?

GEORGE: Annie, why isn't his name on it?

CHRIS: Even when I don't own it!

GEORGE: Who're you kidding? Who gets it when he dies? (*To Ann.*) Open your eyes, you know the both of them, isn't that the first thing they'd do, the way they love each other? – J. O. Keller and Son? (*Pause.* ANN *looks from him to Chris.*) I'll settle it. Do you want to settle it, or are you afraid to?

CHRIS: What do you mean?

GEORGE: Let me go up and talk to your father. In ten minutes you'll have the answer. Or are you afraid of the answer?

CHRIS: I'm not afraid of the answer. I know the answer. But my mother isn't well and I don't want a fight here now.

GEORGE: Let me go to him.

CHRIS: You're not going to start a fight here now.

GEORGE (*to Ann*): What more do you want! (*There is a sound of footsteps in the house.*)

ANN (*turns her head suddenly towards house*): Someone's coming.

CHRIS (*to George, quietly*): You won't say anything now.

ANN: You'll go soon. I'll call a cab.

GEORGE: You're coming with me.

ANN: And don't mention marriage, because we haven't told her yet.

GEORGE: You're coming with me.

ANN: You understand? Don't – George, you're not going to start anything now! (*She hears footsteps.*) Shsh!

> MOTHER *enters on porch. She is dressed almost formally; her hair is fixed. They are all turned towards her. On seeing George she raises both hands, comes down towards him.*

MOTHER: Georgie, Georgie.

GEORGE (*he has always liked her*): Hello, Kate.

MOTHER (*cups his face in her hands*): They made an old man out of you. (*Touches his hair.*) Look, you're grey.

GEORGE (*her pity, open and unabashed, reaches into him, and he smiles sadly*): I know, I —

MOTHER: I told you when you went away, don't try for medals.

GEORGE (*laughs, tiredly*): I didn't try, Kate. They made it very easy for me.

MOTHER (*actually angry*): Go on. You're all alike. (*To Ann.*) Look at him, why did you say he's fine? He looks like a ghost.

GEORGE (*relishing her solicitude*): I feel all right.

MOTHER: I'm sick to look at you. What's the matter with your mother, why don't she feed you?

ANN: He just hasn't any appetite.

MOTHER: If he ate in my house he'd have an appetite. (*To Ann.*) I pity your husband! (*To George.*) Sit down. I'll make you a sandwich.

GEORGE (*sits with an embarrassed laugh*): I'm really not hungry.

MOTHER: Honest to God, it breaks my heart to see what happened to all the children. How we worked and planned for you, and you end up no better than us.

GEORGE (*with deep feeling for her*): You . . . you haven't changed at all, you know that, Kate?

MOTHER: None of us changed, Georgie. We all love you. Joe was just talking about the day you were born and the water got shut off. People were carrying basins from a block away – a stranger would have thought the whole neighbourhood was on fire! (*They laugh. She sees the juice. To Ann.*) Why didn't you give him some juice!

ANN (*defensively*): I offered it to him.

MOTHER (*scoffingly*): You offered it to him! (*Thrusting glass into George's hand.*) Give it to him! (*To George, who is laughing.*) And now you're going to sit here and drink some juice . . . and look like something!

GEORGE (*sitting*): Kate, I feel hungry already.

CHRIS (*proudly*): She could turn Mahatma Ghandi into a heavyweight!

MOTHER (*to Chris, with great energy*): Listen, to hell with the restaurant! I got a ham in the icebox, and frozen strawberries, and avocados, and —

ANN: Swell, I'll help you!

GEORGE: The train leaves at eight-thirty, Ann.

MOTHER (*to Ann*): You're leaving?

CHRIS: No, Mother, she's not —

ANN (*breaking through it, going to George*): You hardly got here; give yourself a chance to get acquainted again.

CHRIS: Sure, you don't even know us any more.

MOTHER: Well, Chris, if they can't stay, don't —

CHRIS: No, it's just a question of George, Mother, he planned on —

GEORGE (*gets up politely, nicely, for Kate's sake*): Now wait a minute, Chris . . .

CHRIS (*smiling and full of command, cutting him off*): If you want to

go, I'll drive you to the station now, but if you're staying, no
arguments while you're here.

MOTHER (*at last confessing the tension*): Why should he argue?
(*She goes to him. With desperation and compassion, stroking his
hair.*) Georgie and us have no argument. How could we have
an argument, Georgie? We all got hit by the same lightning,
how can you —? Did you see what happened to Larry's tree,
Georgie? (*She has taken his arm, and unwillingly he moves across
stage with her.*) Imagine? While I was dreaming of him in the
middle of the night, the wind came along and —

LYDIA *enters on porch. As soon as she sees him:*

LYDIA: Hey, Georgie! Georgie! Georgie! Georgie! Georgie!
(*She comes down to him eagerly. She has a flowered hat in her hand,
which KATE takes from her as she goes to George.*)

GEORGE (*as they shake hands eagerly, warmly*): Hello, Laughy.
What'd you do, grow?

LYDIA: I'm a big girl now.

MOTHER: Look what she can do to a hat!

ANN (*to Lydia, admiring the hat*): Did you make that?

MOTHER: In ten minutes! (*She puts it on.*)

LYDIA (*fixing it on her head*): I only rearranged it.

GEORGE: You still make your own clothes?

CHRIS (*of Mother*): Ain't she classy! All she needs now is a Russian
wolfhound.

MOTHER (*moving her head*): It feels like somebody is sitting on my
head.

ANN: No, it's beautiful, Kate.

MOTHER (*kisses Lydia. To George*): She's a genius! You should've
married her. (*They laugh.*) This one can feed you!

LYDIA (*strangely embarrassed*): Oh, stop that, Kate.

GEORGE (*to Lydia*): Didn't I hear you had a baby?

MOTHER: You don't hear so good. She's got three babies.

GEORGE (*a little hurt by it – to Lydia*): No kidding, three?

LYDIA: Yeah, it was one, two, three – You've been away a long
time, Georgie.

GEORGE: I'm beginning to realize.

MOTHER (*to Chris and George*): The trouble with you kids is you *think* too much.

LYDIA: Well, we think, too.

MOTHER: Yes, but not all the time.

GEORGE (*with almost obvious envy*): They never took Frank, heh?

LYDIA (*a little apologetically*): No, he was always one year ahead of the draft.

MOTHER: It's amazing. When they were calling boys twenty-seven Frank was just twenty-eight, when they made it twenty-eight he was just twenty-nine. That's why he took up astrology. It's all in when you were born, it just goes to show.

CHRIS: What does it go to show?

MOTHER (*to Chris*): Don't be so intelligent. Some superstitions are very nice! (*To Lydia.*) Did he finish Larry's horoscope?

LYDIA: I'll ask him now, I'm going in. (*To George, a little sadly, almost embarrassed.*) Would you like to see my babies? Come on.

GEORGE: I don't think so, Lydia.

LYDIA (*understanding*): All right. Good luck to you, George.

GEORGE: Thanks. And to you . . . And Frank. (*She smiles at him, turns and goes off to her house.* GEORGE *stands staring after her.*)

LYDIA (*as she runs off*): Oh, Frank!

MOTHER (*reading his thoughts*): She got pretty, heh?

GEORGE (*sadly*): Very pretty.

MOTHER (*as a reprimand*): She's beautiful, you damned fool!

GEORGE (*looks around longingly; and softly, with a catch in his throat*): She makes it seem so nice around here.

MOTHER (*shaking her finger at him*): Look what happened to you because you wouldn't listen to me! I told you to marry that girl and stay out of the war!

GEORGE (*laughs at himself*): She used to laugh too much.

MOTHER: And you didn't laugh enough. While you were getting mad about Fascism Frank was getting into her bed.

GEORGE (*to Chris*): He won the war, Frank.

CHRIS: All the battles.

MOTHER (*in pursuit of this mood*): The day they started the draft, Georgie, I told you you loved that girl.

CHRIS (*laughs*): And truer love hath no man!

MOTHER: I'm smarter than any of you.

GEORGIE (*laughing*): She's wonderful!

MOTHER: And now you're going to listen to me, George. You had big principles, Eagle Scouts the three of you; so now I got a tree, and this one – (*indicating Chris*) – when the weather gets bad he can't stand on his feet; and that big dope – (*pointing to Lydia's house*) – next door who never reads anything but Andy Gump has three children and his house paid off. Stop being a philosopher, and look after yourself. Like Joe was just saying – you move back here, he'll help you get set, and I'll find you a girl and put a smile on your face.

GEORGE: Joe? Joe wants me here?

ANN (*eagerly*): He asked me to tell you, and I think it's a good idea.

MOTHER: Certainly. Why must you make believe you hate us? Is that another principle? – that you have to hate us? You don't hate us, George, I know you, you can't fool me, I diapered you. (*Suddenly, to Ann.*) You remember Mr Marcy's daughter?

ANN (*laughing, to George*): She's got you hooked already! (GEORGE *laughs, is excited.*)

MOTHER: You look her over, George; you'll see she's the most beautiful —

CHRIS: She's got warts, George.

MOTHER (*to Chris*): She hasn't got warts! (*To George.*) So the girl has a little beauty mark on her chin —

CHRIS: And two on her nose.

MOTHER: You remember. Her father's the retired police inspector.

CHRIS: Sergeant, George.

MOTHER: He's a very kind man!

CHRIS: He looks like a gorilla.

MOTHER (*to George*): He never shot anybody.

They all burst out laughing, as KELLER *appears in doorway.*
GEORGE *rises abruptly and stares at Keller, who comes rapidly
down to him.*

KELLER (*the laughter stops. With strained joviality*): Well! Look
who's here! (*Extending his hand.*) Georgie, good to see ya.

GEORGE (*shaking hands – sombrely*): How're you, Joe?

KELLER: So-so. Gettin' old. You comin' out to dinner with
us?

GEORGE: No, got to be back in New York.

ANN: I'll call a cab for you. (*She goes up into the house.*)

KELLER: Too bad you can't stay, George. Sit down. (*To Mother.*)
He looks fine.

MOTHER: He looks terrible.

KELLER: That's what I said, you look terrible, George. (*They
laugh.*) I wear the pants and she beats me with the belt.

GEORGE: I saw your factory on the way from the station. It looks
like General Motors.

KELLER: I wish it was General Motors, but it ain't. Sit down,
George. Sit down. (*Takes cigar out of his pocket.*) So you finally
went to see your father, I hear?

GEORGE: Yes, this morning. What kind of stuff do you make
now?

KELLER: Oh, little of everything. Pressure cookers, an assembly
for washing machines. Got a nice, flexible plant now. So how'd
you find Dad? Feel all right?

GEORGE (*searching Keller, speaking indecisively*): No, he's not well,
Joe.

KELLER (*lighting his cigar*): Not his heart again, is it?

GEORGE: It's everything, Joe. It's his soul.

KELLER (*blowing out smoke*): Uh huh —

CHRIS: How about seeing what they did with your house?

KELLER: Leave him be.

GEORGE (*to Chris, indicating Keller*): I'd like to talk to him.

KELLER: Sure, he just got here. That's the way they do, George.
A little man makes a mistake and they hang him by the thumbs;

the big ones become ambassadors. I wish you'd-a told me you
were going to see Dad.

GEORGE (*studying him*): I didn't know you were interested.

KELLER: In a way, I am. I would like him to know, George, that
as far as I'm concerned, any time he wants, he's got a place with
me. I would like him to know that.

GEORGE: He hates your guts, Joe. Don't you know that?

KELLER: I imagined it. But that can change, too.

MOTHER: Steve was never like that.

GEORGE: He's like that now. He'd like to take every man who
made money in the war and put him up against a wall.

CHRIS: He'll need a lot of bullets.

GEORGE: And he'd better not get any.

KELLER: That's a sad thing to hear.

GEORGE (*with bitterness dominant*): Why? What'd you expect him
to think of you?

KELLER (*the force of his nature rising, but under control*): I'm sad to
see he hasn't changed. As long as I know him, twenty-five
years, the man never learned how to take the blame. You know
that, George.

GEORGE (*he does*): Well, I —

KELLER: But you do know it. Because the way you come in here
you don't look like you remember it. I mean like in nineteen
thirty-seven when we had the shop on Flood Street. And he
damn near blew us all up with that heater he left burning for
two days without water. He wouldn't admit that was his fault,
either. I had to fire a mechanic to save his face. You remember
that.

GEORGE: Yes, but —

KELLER: I'm just mentioning it, George. Because this is just
another one of a lot of things. Like when he gave Frank that
money to invest in oil stock.

GEORGE (*distressed*): I know that, I —

KELLER (*driving in, but restrained*): But it's good to remember
those things, kid. The way he cursed Frank because the stock

went down. Was that Frank's fault? To listen to him Frank was a swindler. And all the man did was give him a bad tip.

GEORGE (*gets up, moves away*): I know those things . . .

KELLER: Then remember them, remember them. (ANN *comes out of house.*) There are certain men in the world who rather see everybody hung before they'll take blame. You understand me, George?

They stand facing each other, GEORGE *trying to judge him.*

ANN (*coming downstage*): The cab's on its way. Would you like to wash?

MOTHER (*with the thrust of hope*): Why must he go? Make the midnight, George.

KELLER: Sure, you'll have dinner with us!

ANN: How about it? Why not? We're eating at the lake, we could have a swell time.

A long pause, as GEORGE *looks at Ann, Chris, Keller, then back to her.*

MOTHER: Now you're talking.

CHRIS: I've got a shirt that'll go right with that suit.

MOTHER: Size fifteen and a half, right, George?

GEORGE: Is Lydia —? I mean – Frank and Lydia coming?

MOTHER: I'll get you a date that'll make her look like a — (*She starts upstage.*)

GEORGE (*laughing*): No, I don't want a date.

CHRIS: I know somebody just for you! Charlotte Tanner! (*He starts for the house.*)

KELLER: Call Charlotte, that's right.

MOTHER: Sure, call her up. (CHRIS *goes into house.*)

ANN: You go up and pick out a shirt and tie.

GEORGE (*stops, looks around at them and the place*): I never felt at home anywhere but here. I feel so – (*He nearly laughs, and turns away from them.*) Kate, you look so young, you know? You didn't change at all. It . . . rings an old bell. (*Turns to Keller.*) You too, Joe, you're amazingly the same. The whole atmosphere is.

KELLER: Say, I ain't got time to get sick.

MOTHER: He hasn't been laid up in fifteen years.

KELLER: Except my flu during the war.

MOTHER: Huhh?

KELLER: My flu, when I was sick during . . . the war.

MOTHER: Well, sure . . . (*To George.*) I mean except for that flu. (GEORGE *stands perfectly still.*) Well, it slipped my mind. Don't look at me that way. He wanted to go to the shop but he couldn't lift himself off the bed. I thought he had pneumonia.

GEORGE: Why did you say he's never— ?

KELLER: I know how you feel, kid. I'll never forgive myself. If I could've gone in that day I'd never allow Dad to touch those heads.

GEORGE: She said you've never been sick.

MOTHER: I said he was sick, George.

GEORGE (*going to Ann*): Ann, didn't you hear her say —?

MOTHER: Do you remember every time you were sick?

GEORGE: I'd remember pneumonia. Especially if I got it just the day my partner was going to patch up cylinder heads . . . What happened that day, Joe?

   FRANK *enters briskly from driveway, holding Larry's horoscope in his hand. He comes to Kate.*

FRANK: Kate! Kate!

MOTHER: Frank, did you see George?

FRANK (*extending his hand*): Lydia told me, I'm glad to . . . you'll have to pardon me. (*Pulling Mother over*) I've got something amazing for you, Kate, I finished Larry's horoscope.

MOTHER: You'd be interested in this, George. It's wonderful the way he can understand the —

CHRIS (*entering from house*): George, the girl's on the phone —

MOTHER (*desperately*): He finished Larry's horoscope!

CHRIS: Frank, can't you pick a better time than this?

FRANK: The greatest men who ever lived believed in the stars!

CHRIS: Stop filling her head with that junk!

FRANK: Is it junk to feel that there's a greater power than our-
selves? I've studied the stars of his life! I won't argue with you,
I'm telling you. Somewhere in this world your brother is
alive!

MOTHER (*instantly to Chris*): Why isn't it possible?

CHRIS: Because it's insane.

FRANK: Just a minute now. I'll tell you something and you can
do as you please. Just let me say it. He was supposed to have
died on November twenty-fifth. But November twenty-fifth
was his favourable day.

CHRIS: Mother!

MOTHER: Listen to him!

FRANK: It was a day when everything good was shining on him,
the kind of day he should've married on. You can laugh at a lot
of it. I can understand you laughing. But the odds are a million
to one that a man won't die on his favourable day. That's
known, that's known, Chris!

MOTHER: Why isn't it possible, why isn't it possible, Chris!

GEORGE (*to Ann*): Don't you understand what she's saying? She
just told you to go. What are you waiting for now?

CHRIS: Nobody can tell her to go. (*A car horn is heard.*)

MOTHER (*to Frank*): Thank you, darling, for your trouble. Will
you tell him to wait, Frank?

FRANK (*as he goes*): Sure thing.

MOTHER (*calling out*): They'll be right out, driver!

CHRIS: She's not leaving, Mother.

GEORGE: You heard her say it, he's never been sick!

MOTHER: He misunderstood me, Chris! (CHRIS *looks at her,
struck.*)

GEORGE (*to Ann*): He simply told your father to kill pilots, and
covered himself in bed!

CHRIS: You'd better answer him, Annie. Answer him.

MOTHER: I packed your bag, darling.

CHRIS: What?

MOTHER: I packed your bag. All you've got to do is close it.

ANN: I'm not closing anything. He asked me here and I'm staying till he tells me to go. (*To George.*) Till Chris tells me!

CHRIS: That's all! Now get out of here, George!

MOTHER (*to Chris*): But if that's how he feels —

CHRIS: That's all, nothing more till Christ comes, about the case or Larry as long as I'm here! (*To George.*) Now get out of here, George!

GEORGE (*to Ann*): You tell me. I want to hear you tell me.

ANN: Go, George!

> *They disappear up the driveway,* ANN *saying, 'Don't take it that way, Georgie! Please don't take it that way.'*

CHRIS (*turning to his mother*): What do you mean, you packed her bag? How dare you pack her bag?

MOTHER: Chris —

CHRIS: How dare you pack her bag?

MOTHER: She doesn't belong here.

CHRIS: Then I don't belong here.

MOTHER: She's Larry's girl.

CHRIS: And I'm his brother and he's dead, and I'm marrying his girl.

MOTHER: Never, never in this world!

KELLER: You lost your mind?

MOTHER: You have nothing to say!

KELLER (*cruelly*): I got plenty to say. Three and a half years you been talking like a maniac —

> MOTHER *smashes him across the face.*

MOTHER: Nothing. You have nothing to say. Now I say. He's coming back, and everybody has got to wait.

CHRIS: Mother, Mother —

MOTHER: Wait, wait —

CHRIS: How long? How long?

MOTHER (*rolling out of her*): Till he comes; forever and ever till he comes!

CHRIS (*as an ultimatum*): Mother, I'm going ahead with it.

MOTHER: Chris, I've never said no to you in my life, now I say no!

CHRIS: You'll never let him go till I do it.

MOTHER: I'll never let him go and you'll never let him go!

CHRIS: I've let him go. I've let him go a long —

MOTHER (*with no less force, but turning from him*): Then let your father go. (*Pause.* CHRIS *stands transfixed.*)

KELLER: She's out of her mind.

MOTHER: Altogether! (*To Chris, but not facing them.*) Your brother's alive, darling, because if he's dead, your father killed him. Do you understand me now? As long as you live, that boy is alive. God does not let a son be killed by his father. Now you see, don't you? Now you see. (*Beyond control, she hurries up and into house.*)

KELLER (CHRIS *has not moved. He speaks insinuatingly, questioningly*): She's out of her mind.

CHRIS (*in a broken whisper*): Then . . . you did it?

KELLER (*with the beginning of plea in his voice*): He never flew a P-40 —

CHRIS (*struck; deadly*): But the others.

KELLER (*insistently*): She's out of her mind. (*He takes a step towards Chris, pleadingly.*)

CHRIS (*unyielding*): Dad . . . you did it?

KELLER: He never flew a P-40, what's the matter with you?

CHRIS (*still asking, and saying*): Then you did it. To the others.
    Both hold their voices down.

KELLER (*afraid of him, his deadly insistence*): What's the matter with you? What the hell is the matter with you?

CHRIS (*quietly, incredibly*): How could you do that? How?

KELLER: What's the matter with you!

CHRIS: Dad . . . Dad, you killed twenty-one men!

KELLER: What, killed?

CHRIS: You killed them, you murdered them.

KELLER (*as though throwing his whole nature open before Chris*): How could I kill anybody?

CHRIS: Dad! Dad!

KELLER (*trying to hush him*): I didn't kill anybody!

CHRIS: Then explain it to me. What did you do? Explain it to me or I'll tear you to pieces!

KELLER (*horrified at his overwhelming fury*): Don't, Chris, don't —

CHRIS: I want to know what you did, now what did you do? You had a hundred and twenty cracked engine-heads, now what did you do?

KELLER: If you're going to hang me then I —

CHRIS: I'm listening. God Almighty, I'm listening!

KELLER (*their movements now are those of subtle pursuit and escape. KELLER keeps a step out of Chris's range as he talks*): You're a boy, what could I do! I'm in business, a man is in business; a hundred and twenty cracked, you're out of business; you got a process, the process don't work you're out of business; you don't know how to operate, your stuff is no good; they close you up, they tear up your contracts, what the hell's it to them? You lay forty years into a business and they knock you out in five minutes, what could I do, let them take forty years, let them take my life away? (*His voice cracking.*) I never thought they'd install them. I swear to God. I thought they'd stop 'em before anybody took off.

CHRIS: Then why'd you ship them out?

KELLER: By the time they could spot them I thought I'd have the process going again, and I could show them they needed me and they'd let it go by. But weeks passed and I got no kick-back, so I was going to tell them.

CHRIS: Then why didn't you tell them?

KELLER: It was too late. The paper, it was all over the front page, twenty-one went down, it was too late. They came with hand-cuffs into the shop, what could I do? (*He sits on bench.*) Chris . . . Chris, I did it for you, it was a chance and I took it for you. I'm sixty-one years old, when would I have another chance to make something for you? Sixty-one years old you don't get another chance, do ya?

CHRIS: You even knew they wouldn't hold up in the air.

KELLER: I didn't say that.

CHRIS: But you were going to warn them not to use them —

KELLER: But that don't mean —

CHRIS: It means you knew they'd crash.

KELLER: It don't mean that.

CHRIS: Then you *thought* they'd crash.

KELLER: I was afraid maybe —

CHRIS: You were afraid maybe! God in heaven, what kind of a man are you? Kids were hanging in the air by those heads. You knew that!

KELLER: For you, a business for you!

CHRIS (*with burning fury*): For me! Where do you live, where have you come from? For me! – I was dying every day and you were killing my boys and you did it for me? What the hell do you think I was thinking of, the Goddam business? Is that as far as your mind can see, the business? What is that, the world – the business? What the hell do you mean, you did it for me? Don't you have a country? Don't you live in the world? What the hell are you? You're not even an animal, no animal kills his own, what are yon? What must I do to you? I ought to tear the tongue out of your mouth, what must I do? (*With his fist he pounds down upon his father's shoulder. He stumbles away, covering his face as he weeps.*) What must I do, Jesus God, what must I do?

KELLER: Chris . . . My Chris . . .

CURTAIN

ACT THREE

Two o'clock the following morning, MOTHER is discovered on the rise rocking ceaselessly in a chair, staring at her thoughts. It is an intense, slight, sort of rocking. A light shows from upstairs bedroom, lower floor windows being dark. The moon is strong and casts its bluish light.

Presently JIM, dressed in jacket and hat, appears, and seeing her, goes up beside her.

JIM: Any news?

MOTHER: No news.

JIM *(gently)*: You can't sit up all night, dear, why don't you go to bed?

MOTHER: I'm waiting for Chris. Don't worry about me, Jim, I'm perfectly all right.

JIM: But it's almost two o'clock.

MOTHER: I can't sleep. *(Slight pause.)* You had an emergency?

JIM *(tiredly)*: Somebody had a headache and thought he was dying. *(Slight pause.)* Half of my patients are quite mad. Nobody realizes how many people are walking around loose, and they're cracked as coconuts. Money. Money-money-money-money. You say it long enough it doesn't mean anything. *(She smiles, makes a silent laugh.)* Oh, how I'd love to be around when that happens!

MOTHER *(shaking her head)*: You're so childish, Jim! Sometimes you are.

JIM *(looks at her a moment)*: Kate. *(Pause.)* What happened?

MOTHER: I told you. He had an argument with Joe. Then he got in the car and drove away.

JIM: What kind of an argument?

MOTHER: An argument, Joe . . . He was crying like a child, before.

JIM: They argued about Ann?

MOTHER (*after slight hesitation*): No, not Ann. Imagine? (*Indicates lighted window above.*) She hasn't come out of that room since he left. All night in that room.

JIM (*looks at window, then at her*): What'd Joe do, tell him?

MOTHER (*stops rocking*): Tell him what?

JIM: Don't be afraid, Kate, I know. I've always known.

MOTHER: How?

JIM: It occurred to me a long time ago.

MOTHER: I always had the feeling that in the back of his head, Chris . . . almost knew. I didn't think it would be such a shock.

JIM (*gets up*): Chris would never know how to live with a thing like that. It takes a certain talent – for lying. You have it, and I do. But not him.

MOTHER: What do you mean . . . He's not coming back?

JIM: Oh, no, he'll come back. We all come back, Kate. These private little revolutions always die. The compromise is always made. In a peculiar way, Frank is right – every man does have a star. The star of one's honesty. And you spend your life groping for it, but once it's out it never lights again. I don't think he went very far. He probably just wanted to be alone to watch his star go out.

MOTHER: Just as long as he comes back.

JIM: I wish he wouldn't, Kate. One year I simply took off, went to New Orleans; for two months I lived on bananas and milk, and studied a certain disease. It was beautiful. And then she came, and she cried. And I went back home with her. And now I live in the usual darkness; I can't find myself; it's even hard sometimes to remember the kind of man I wanted to be. I'm a good husband; Chris is a good son – he'll come back.

KELLER *comes out on porch in dressing gown and slippers. He goes upstage – to alley.* JIM *goes to him.*

JIM: I have a feeling he's in the park. I'll look around for him. Put her to bed, Joe; this is no good for what she's got. (JIM *exits up driveway*.)

KELLER (*coming down*): What does he want here?

MOTHER: His friend is not home.

KELLER (*comes down to her. His voice is husky*): I don't like him mixing in so much.

MOTHER: It's too late, Joe. He knows.

KELLER (*apprehensively*): How does he know?

MOTHER: He guessed a long time ago.

KELLER: I don't like that.

MOTHER (*laughs dangerously, quietly into the line*): What you don't like.

KELLER: Yeah, what I don't like.

MOTHER: You can't bull yourself through this one, Joe, you better be smart now. This thing – this thing is not over yet.

KELLER (*indicating lighted window above*): And what is she doing up there? She don't come out of the room.

MOTHER: I don't know, what is she doing? Sit down, stop being mad. You want to live? You better figure out your life.

KELLER: She don't know, does she?

MOTHER: She saw Chris storming out of here. It's one and one – she knows how to add.

KELLER: Maybe I ought to talk to her?

MOTHER: Don't ask me, Joe.

KELLER (*almost an outburst*): Then who do I ask? But I don't think she'll do anything about it.

MOTHER: You're asking me again.

KELLER: I'm askin' you. What am I, a stranger? I thought I had a family here. What happened to my family?

MOTHER: You've got a family. I'm simply telling you that I have no strength to think any more.

KELLER: You have no strength. The minute there's trouble you have no strength.

MOTHER: Joe, you're doing the same thing again; all your life whenever there's trouble you yell at me and you think that settles it.

KELLER: Then what do I do? Tell me, talk to me, what do I do?

MOTHER: Joe . . . I've been thinking this way. If he comes back —

KELLER: What do you mean 'if'? He's comin' back!

MOTHER: I think if you sit him down and you – explain yourself. I mean you ought to make it clear to him that you know you did a terrible thing. (*Not looking into his eyes.*) I mean if he saw that you realize what you did. You see?

KELLER: What ice does that cut?

MOTHER (*a little fearfully*): I mean if you told him that you want to pay for what you did.

KELLER (*sensing . . . quietly*): How can I pay?

MOTHER: Tell him – you're willing to go to prison. (*Pause.*)

KELLER (*struck, amazed*): I'm willing to —?

MOTHER (*quickly*): You wouldn't go, he wouldn't ask you to go. But if you told him you wanted to, if he could feel that you wanted to pay, maybe he would forgive you.

KELLER: He would forgive me! For what?

MOTHER: Joe, you know what I mean.

KELLER: I don't know what you mean! You wanted money, so I made money. What must I be forgiven? You wanted money, didn't you?

MOTHER: I didn't want it that way.

KELLER: I didn't want it that way, either! What difference is it what you want? I spoiled the both of you. I should've put him out when he was ten like I was put out, and make him earn his keep. Then he'd know how a buck is made in this world. Forgiven! I could live on a quarter a day myself, but I got a family so I —

MOTHER: Joe, Joe . . . It don't excuse it that you did it for the family.

KELLER: It's got to excuse it!

MOTHER: There's something bigger than the family to him.

KELLER: Nothin' is bigger!

MOTHER: There is to him.

KELLER: There's nothin' he could do that I wouldn't forgive. Because he's my son. Because I'm his father and he's my son.

MOTHER: Joe, I tell you —

KELLER: Nothin's bigger than that. And you're goin' to tell him, you understand? I'm his father and he's my son, and if there's something bigger than that I'll put a bullet in my head!

MOTHER: You stop that!

KELLER: You heard me. Now you know what to tell him. (*Pause. He moves from her – halts.*) But he wouldn't put me away though . . . He wouldn't do that . . . Would he?

MOTHER: He loved you, Joe, you broke his heart.

KELLER: But to put me away . . .

MOTHER: I don't know. I'm beginning to think we don't really know him. They say in the war he was such a killer. Here he was always afraid of mice. I don't know him. I don't know what he'll do.

KELLER: Goddam, if Larry was alive he wouldn't act like this. He understood the way the world is made. He listened to me. To him the world had a forty-foot front, it ended at the building line. This one, everything bothers him. You make a deal, overcharge two cents, and his hair falls out. He don't understand money. Too easy, it came too easy. Yes, sir. Larry. That was a boy we lost. Larry. Larry. (*He slumps on chair in front of her.*) What am I gonna do, Kate?

MOTHER: Joe, Joe, please . . . You'll be all right, nothing is going to happen.

KELLER (*desperately, lost*): For you, Kate, for both of you, that's all I ever lived for . . .

MOTHER: I know, darling, I know. (ANN *enters from house. They say nothing, waiting for her to speak.*)

ANN: Why do you stay up? I'll tell you when he comes.

KELLER (*rises, goes to her*): You didn't eat supper, did you? (*To Mother.*) Why don't you make her something?

MOTHER: Sure, I'll —

ANN: Never mind, Kate, I'm all right. (*They are unable to speak to each other.*) There's something I want to tell you. (*She starts, then halts.*) I'm not going to do anything about it.

MOTHER: She's a good girl! (*To Keller.*) You see? She's a —

ANN: I'll do nothing about Joe, but you're going to do something for me. (*Directly to Mother.*) You made Chris feel guilty with me. Whether you wanted to or not, you've crippled him in front of me. I'd like you to tell him that Larry is dead and that you know it. You understand me? I'm not going out of here alone. There's no life for me that way. I want you to set him free. And then I promise you, everything will end, and we'll go away, and that's all.

KELLER: You'll do that. You'll tell him.

ANN: I know what I'm asking, Kate. You had two sons. But you've only got one now.

KELLER: You'll tell him.

ANN: And you've got to say it to him so he knows you mean it.

MOTHER: My dear, if the boy was dead, it wouldn't depend on my words to make Chris know it. . . . The night he gets into your bed, his heart will dry up. Because he knows and you know. To his dying day he'll wait for his brother! No, my dear, no such thing. You're going in the morning, and you're going alone. That's your life, that's your lonely life. (*She goes to porch, and starts in.*)

ANN: Larry is dead, Kate.

MOTHER (*she stops*): Don't speak to me.

ANN: I said he's dead. I know! He crashed off the coast of China November twenty-fifth! His engine didn't fail him. But he died. I know . . .

MOTHER: How did he die? You're lying to me. If you know, how did he die?

ANN: I loved him. You know I loved him. Would I have looked at anyone else if I wasn't sure? That's enough for you.

MOTHER (*moving on her*): What's enough for me? What're you talking about? (*She grasps Ann's wrists.*)

ANN: You're hurting my wrists.

MOTHER: What are you talking about! (*Pause. She stares at Ann a moment, then turns and goes to Keller.*)

ANN: Joe, go in the house.

KELLER: Why should I —

ANN: Please go.

KELLER: Lemme know when he comes. (*Keller goes into house.*)

MOTHER (*as she sees* ANN *taking a letter from her pocket*): What's that?

ANN: Sit down. (*Mother moves left to chair, but does not sit.*) First you've got to understand. When I came, I didn't have any idea that Joe – I had nothing against him or you. I came to get married. I hoped . . . So I didn't bring this to hurt you. I thought I'd show it to you only if there was no other way to settle Larry in your mind.

MOTHER: Larry? (*Snatches letter from Ann's hand.*)

ANN: He wrote it to me just before he — (MOTHER *opens and begins to read letter.*) I'm not trying to hurt you, Kate. You're making me do this, now remember you're — Remember. I've been so lonely, Kate . . . I can't leave here alone again. (*A long, low moan comes from* MOTHER's *throat as she reads.*) You made me show it to you. You wouldn't believe me. I told you a hundred times, why wouldn't you believe me!

MOTHER: Oh, my God . . .

ANN (*with pity and fear*): Kate, please, please . . .

MOTHER: My God, my God . . .

ANN: Kate, dear, I'm so sorry . . . I'm so sorry.

CHRIS *enters from driveway. He seems exhausted.*

CHRIS: What's the matter —?

ANN: Where were you? . . . You're all perspired. (MOTHER *doesn't move.*) Where were you?

CHRIS: Just drove around a little. I thought you'd be gone.

ANN: Where do I go? I have nowhere to go.

CHRIS (*to Mother*): Where's Dad?

ANN: Inside, lying down.

CHRIS: Sit down, both of you. I'll say what there is to say.

MOTHER: I didn't hear the car . . .

CHRIS: I left it in the garage.

MOTHER: Jim is out looking for you.

CHRIS: Mother . . . I'm going away. There are a couple of firms in Cleveland, I think I can get a place. I mean, I'm going away for good. (*To Ann alone.*) I know what you're thinking, Annie. It's true. I'm yellow. I was made yellow in this house because I suspected my father and I did nothing about it, but if I knew that night when I came home what I know now, he'd be in the district attorney's office by this time, and I'd have brought him there. Now if I look at him, all I'm able to do is cry.

MOTHER: What are you talking about? What else can you do?

CHRIS: I could jail him! I could jail him, if I were human any more. But I'm like everybody else now. I'm practical now. You made me practical.

MOTHER: But you have to be.

CHRIS: The cats in that alley are practical, the bums who ran away when we were fighting were practical. Only the dead one's weren't practical. But now I'm practical, and I spit on myself. I'm going away. I'm going now.

ANN (*going up to him*): I'm coming with you.

CHRIS: No, Ann.

ANN: Chris, I don't ask you to do anything about Joe.

CHRIS: You do, you do.

ANN: I swear I never will.

CHRIS: In your heart you always will.

ANN: Then do what you have to do!

CHRIS: Do what? What is there to do? I've looked all night for a reason to make him suffer.

ANN: There's reason, there's reason!

CHRIS: What? Do I raise the dead when I put him behind bars? Then what'll I do it for? We used to shoot a man who acted like a dog, but honour was real there, you were protecting

something. But here? This is the land of the great big dogs, you
don't love a man here, you eat him! That's the principle; the
only one we live by – it just happened to kill a few people this
time, that's all. The world's that way, how can I take it out on
him? What sense does that make? This is a zoo, a zoo!

ANN (*to Mother*): You know what he's got to do? Tell him!

MOTHER: Let him go.

ANN: I won't let him go. You'll tell him what he's got to do . . .

MOTHER: Annie!

ANN: Then I will!

    KELLER *enters from house.* CHRIS *sees him, goes down near
arbour.*

KELLER: What's the matter with you? I want to talk to you.

CHRIS: I've got nothing to say to you.

KELLER (*taking his arm*): I want to talk to you!

CHRIS (*pulling violently away from him*): Don't do that, Dad. I'm
going to hurt you if you do that. There's nothing to say, so say
it quick.

KELLER: Exactly what's the matter? What's the matter? You got
too much money? Is that what bothers you?

CHRIS (*with an edge of sarcasm*): It bothers me.

KELLER: If you can't get used to it, then throw it away. You hear
me? Take every cent and give it to charity, throw it in the
sewer. Does that settle it? In the sewer, that's all. You think I'm
kidding? I'm tellin' you what to do, if it's dirty then burn it.
It's your money, that's not my money. I'm a dead man, I'm an
old dead man, nothing's mine. Well, talk to me! What do
you want to do!

CHRIS: It's not what I want to do. It's what you want to do.

KELLER: What should I want to do? (CHRIS *is silent.*) Jail? You
want me to go to jail? If you want me to go, say so! Is that
where I belong? Then tell me so! (*Slight pause.*) What's the
matter, why can't you tell me? (*Furiously.*) You say everything
else to me, say that! (*Slight pause.*) I'll tell you why you can't
say it. Because you know I don't belong there. Because you

know! (*With growing emphasis and passion, and a persistent tone of desperation.*) Who worked for nothin' in that war? When they work for nothin', I'll work for nothin'. Did they ship a gun or a truck outa Detroit before they got their price? Is that clean? It's dollars and cents, nickels and dimes; war and peace, it's nickels and dimes. What's clean? Half the Goddam country is gotta go if I go! That's why you can't tell me.

CHRIS: That's exactly why.

KELLER: Then . . . why am *I* bad?

CHRIS: *I* know you're no worse than most men but I thought you were better. I never saw you as a man. I saw you as my father. (*Almost breaking.*) I can't look at you this way, I can't look at myself!

He turns away, unable to face Keller. ANN *goes quickly to Mother, takes letter from her and starts for Chris.* MOTHER *instantly rushes to intercept her.*

MOTHER: Give me that!

ANN: He's going to read it! (*She thrusts letter into Chris's hand.*) Larry. He wrote it to me the day he died.

KELLER: Larry!

MOTHER: Chris, it's not for you. (*He starts to read.*) Joe . . . go away . . .

KELLER (*mystified, frightened*): Why'd she say, Larry, what —?

MOTHER (*desperately pushes him towards alley, glancing at Chris*): Go to the street, Joe, go to the street! (*She comes down beside Keller.*) Don't, Chris . . . (*Pleading from her whole soul.*) Don't tell him.

CHRIS (*quietly*): Three and one half years . . . talking, talking. Now you tell me what you must do. . . . This is how he died, now tell me where you belong.

KELLER (*pleading*): Chris, a man can't be a Jesus in this world!

CHRIS: I know all about the world. I know the whole crap story. Now listen to this, and tell me what a man's got to be! (*Reads.*) 'My dear Ann: . . .' You listening? He wrote this the day he died. Listen, don't cry. . . . Listen! 'My dear Ann: It is

impossible to put down the things I feel. But I've got to tell
you something. Yesterday they flew in a load of papers from
the States and I read about Dad and your father being con-
victed. I can't express myself. I can't tell you how I feel – I
can't bear to live any more. Last night I circled the base for
twenty minutes before I could bring myself in. How could he
have done that? Every day three or four men never come back
and he sits back there doing business. . . . I don't know how to
tell you what I feel. . . . I can't face anybody. . . . I'm going out
on a mission in a few minutes. They'll probably report me
missing. If they do, I want you to know that you mustn't wait
for me. I tell you, Ann, if I had him there now I could kill
him —'

(KELLER *grabs letter from Chris's hand and reads it. After a long
pause.*) Now blame the world. Do you understand that letter?

KELLER (*speaking almost inaudibly*): I think I do. Get the car. I'll
put on my jacket. (*He turns and starts slowly for the house.*
MOTHER *rushes to intercept him.*)

MOTHER: Why are you going? You'll sleep, why are you going?

KELLER: I can't sleep here. I'll feel better if I go.

MOTHER: You're so foolish. Larry was your son too, wasn't he?
You know he'd never tell you to do this.

KELLER (*looking at letter in his hand*): Then what is this if it isn't
telling me? Sure, he was my son. But I think to him they were
all my sons. And I guess they were, I guess they were. I'll be
right down. (*Exits into house.*)

MOTHER (*to Chris, with determination*): You're not going to take
him!

CHRIS: I'm taking him.

MOTHER: It's up to you, if you tell him to stay he'll stay. Go and
tell him!

CHRIS: Nobody could stop him now.

MOTHER: You'll stop him! How long will he live in prison? Are
you trying to kill him?

CHRIS (*holding out letter*): I thought you read this!

MOTHER (*of Larry, the letter*): The war is over! Didn't you hear?
It's over!

CHRIS: Then what was Larry to you? A stone that fell into the
water? It's not enough for him to be sorry. Larry didn't kill
himself to make you and Dad sorry.

MOTHER: What more can we be!

CHRIS: You can be better! Once and for all you can know there's
a universe of people outside and you're responsible to it, and
unless you know that, you threw away your son, because that's
why he died.

   A shot is heard in the house. They stand frozen for a brief second.
CHRIS *starts for porch, pauses at step, turns to Ann.*

CHRIS: Find Jim! (*He goes on into the house and* ANN *runs up
driveway.* MOTHER *stands alone, transfixed.*)

MOTHER (*softly, almost moaning*): Joe . . . Joe . . . Joe . . . Joe . . .
(CHRIS *comes out of house, down to Mother's arms.*)

CHRIS (*almost crying*): Mother, I didn't mean to —

MOTHER: Don't, dear. Don't take it on yourself. Forget now. Live.
(CHRIS *stirs as if to answer.*) Shhh . . . (*She puts his arm down
gently and moves towards porch.*) Shhh . . . (*As she reaches porch
steps she begins sobbing.*)

CURTAIN